DISCARD

MAR 14

WILD WORLD

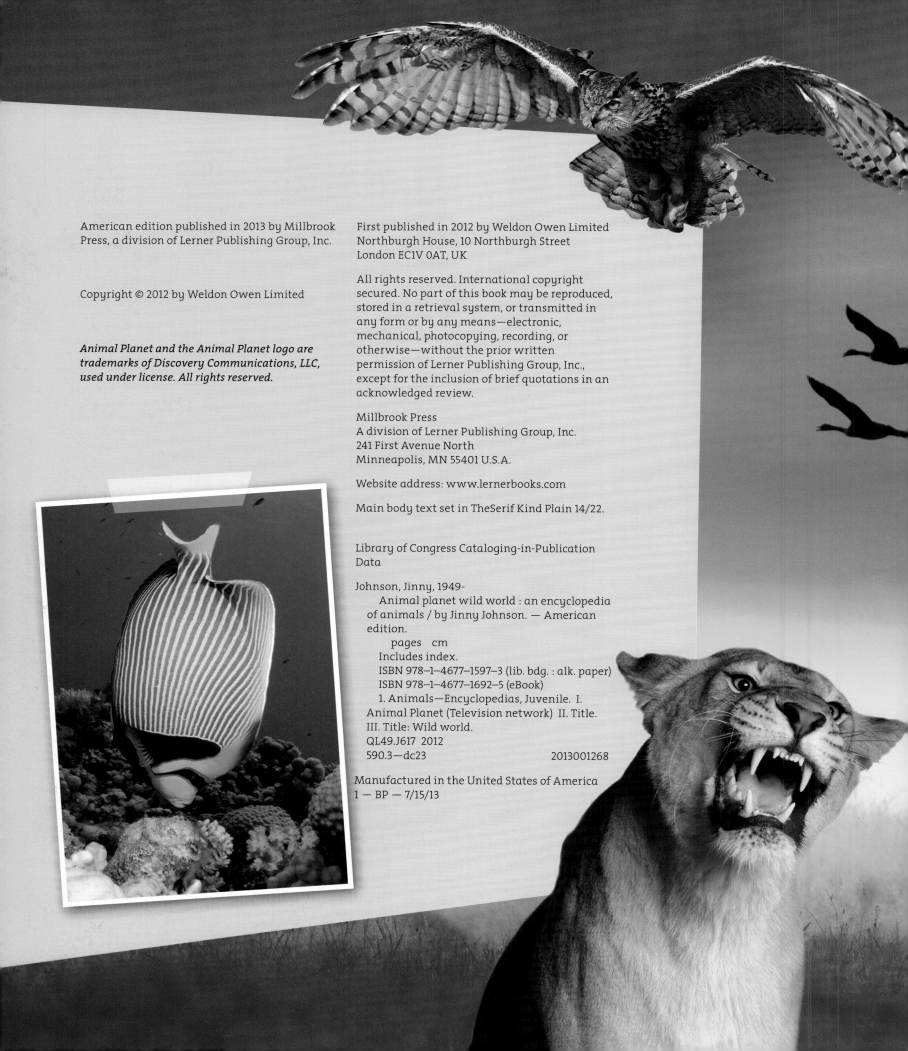

American edition published in 2013 by Millbrook Press, a division of Lerner Publishing Group, Inc.

Copyright © 2012 by Weldon Owen Limited

First published in 2012 by Weldon Owen Limited
Northburgh House, 10 Northburgh Street
London EC1V 0AT, UK

Millbrook Press
A division of Lerner Publishing Group, Inc.
241 First Avenue North
Minneapolis, MN 55401 U.S.A.

Website address: www.lernerbooks.com

Main body text set in TheSerif Kind Plain 14/22.

Library of Congress Cataloging-in-Publication Data

Johnson, Jinny, 1949-
    Animal planet wild world : an encyclopedia of animals / by Jinny Johnson. — American edition.
        pages   cm
    Includes index.
    ISBN 978–1–4677–1597–3 (lib. bdg. : alk. paper)
    ISBN 978–1–4677–1692–5 (eBook)
    1. Animals—Encyclopedias, Juvenile. I. Animal Planet (Television network) II. Title. III. Title: Wild world.
    QL49.J617 2012
    590.3—dc23   2013001268

Manufactured in the United States of America
1 — BP — 7/15/13

WILD WORLD

Jinny Johnson

AN ENCYCLOPEDIA OF ANIMALS

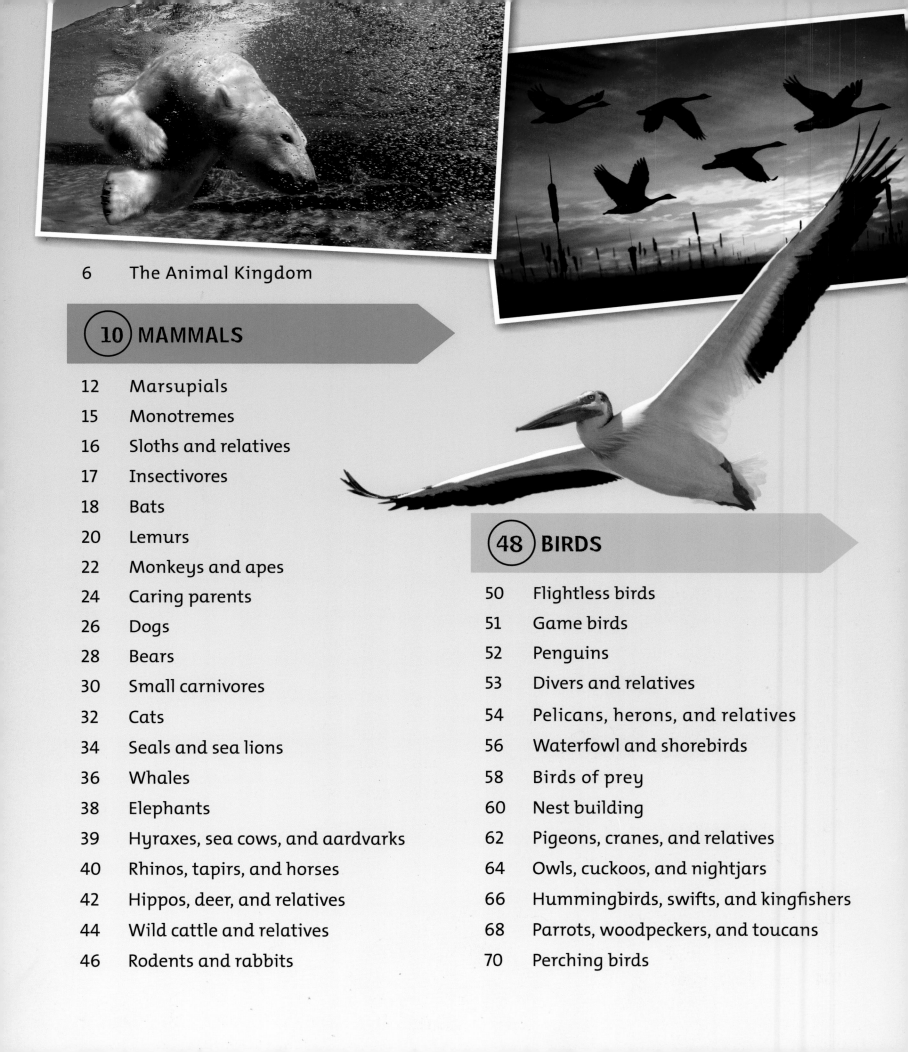

The Animal Kingdom

The natural world is divided into groups called kingdoms, one of which is the Animal Kingdom. This includes all living creatures, from the tiniest worm to blue whales and elephants. However different they may be, all animals are made up of many cells and survive by taking in food. Most can move at least part of themselves. There are two main groups of animals—the vertebrates, which include mammals, birds, reptiles, amphibians, and fish, and the invertebrates, such as insects and spiders. Scientists believe there are many more invertebrates still to be discovered.

Mammals

There are about 5,500 species of mammals in the world, although this number changes as animals become extinct or, occasionally, new species are discovered. Mammals come in a huge variety of shapes and sizes, but all are warm-blooded and have a bony skeleton and lungs to breathe air. Most have a covering of hair or fur. Female mammals feed their young on milk from their own bodies.

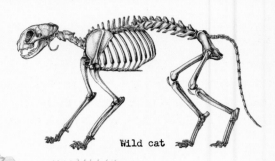

Wild cat

Whale

Egg-laying mammal (echidna)

Marsupial mammal (kangaroo)

Placental mammal (gorilla)

Skeletons

All mammal skeletons have the same basic parts, adapted to suit different lifestyles. For example, in whales the front leg bones support flippers.

Types of mammals

Most mammals give birth to live young that have been nurtured in the mother's body by an organ called the placenta. Marsupials give birth to very small young that finish their development in the mother's pouch. The echidna and the platypus lay eggs.

Senses

Mammals rely on their well-developed senses to help them find food and avoid danger. All of a wolf's senses are good, but it has a particularly keen sense of smell that helps it sniff out prey.

Young zebra feeding on mother's milk

Describing the natural world

Scientists have ways of describing the natural world to help our understanding of the relationships between living things. The Animal Kingdom is divided into groups called phyla. These in turn are split into classes, which contain a number of orders. Each order contains families of related animals, each of which belong to a particular genus. Here's how one creature—the polar bear—is classified.

KINGDOM: Animalia—contains all the animals in the world

PHYLUM: Chordata—animals that have a backbone or nerve cord running down the back of the body

CLASS: Mammalia—warm-blooded vertebrates (animals with a backbone) that have a covering of hair. Female mammals feed their young with milk from their own body.

ORDER: Carnivora—animals that feed mostly on meat and have teeth for biting flesh

FAMILY: Ursidae—bears, the largest land carnivores

GENUS: Ursus—black, brown, and polar bears

SPECIES: Ursus maritimus—the polar bear is the biggest, most predatory bear

Birds

There are nearly 10,000 species of birds, and they live all over the world. A bird is warm-blooded and has two legs, a pair of wings, and a beak. Its body is covered with feathers—birds are the only animals that have feathers. All birds lay eggs, which must be kept warm until they hatch.

Penguin

Hummingbird

Falcon

Adaptable body plan

All birds are similar in structure, but the body plan is adapted for different ways of life, such as soaring flight and killing prey (falcon), hovering to feed on nectar (hummingbird), or swimming (penguin).

Typical bird

Skeleton

Most birds have a light skeleton so the bird can fly. To reduce the weight, the bones are not solid but have a honeycomb-like structure.

Flamingo

Macaw

Beak shapes

Birds' beaks vary according to the food they eat, and there is a huge range of shapes. A macaw's heavy beak is for cracking hard nuts, while a flamingo uses its long, curving beak for filtering small items of food from the water.

Inside an egg

A growing baby bird feeds on the egg yolk and white, and the white also protects it from harm. The egg is enclosed by a hard shell to keep the contents safe.

Embryo starts to grow.

Feeding on egg yolk

Developing chick

About to hatch

Reptiles

There are more than 9,000 species of reptiles, the majority of which live in warm parts of the world. Reptiles are cold-blooded and have a body covering of waterproof scales. Some, but not all, have four legs. Most reptiles lay eggs that have a tough shell, but some give birth to live young.

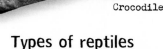
Crocodile

Types of reptiles

The main groups of reptiles are turtles and tortoises, lizards and snakes, and crocodiles. There is also a fourth group with only two species of lizardlike creatures called tuataras.

Tuatara at the entrance to its burrow

Lizard

Tortoise

Snake

Fish

Fish are vertebrates, and there are more species of fish than any other vertebrate animal—at least 31,000. They are cold-blooded, they live in water, and they have fins and tails to help them move and gills for taking oxygen from the water. Most fish lay eggs into the water and leave them to develop and hatch on their own.

Bony fish skeleton

Skeleton

A bony fish has a skull and a backbone like other vertebrates but has fins instead of legs. Many have lots of small bones inside the fins to support them.

Cartilaginous fish (shark)

Bony fish (lyretail)

Types of fish

The cartilaginous fish, which include sharks and rays, have skeletons made of gristly cartilage, not bone. The largest group is the bony fish, with skeletons of bone. The other type of fish is the jawless fish. These fish do not have proper jaws, just suckerlike mouths.

Jawless fish (lamprey)

Amphibians

There are more than 6,000 species of amphibians but many are in danger of extinction, while new species are still being discovered. Amphibians were the first vertebrates to live on land, and most still must spend at least part of their lives in water. Nearly all lay their eggs in water.

Caecilian

Types of amphibians

There are three groups of amphibians: wormlike caecilians, newts and salamanders, and frogs and toads. All are cold-blooded.

Frog skeleton

Skeleton

A frog has long leg bones and a short backbone, which help it jump. Unlike other vertebrates, it has no ribs.

Salamander

Frog

Invertebrates

An invertebrate animal is one without a backbone, and there are far more invertebrates on Earth than any other kind of animal. They live in the water, in the air, on land, and even on Antarctica. Insects are one type of invertebrate, and there are more than a million species, with many more yet to be discovered and named.

Butterfly

Dragonfly

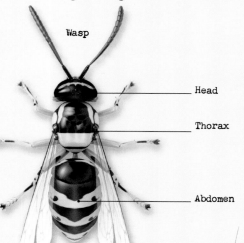

Wasp

Head

Thorax

Abdomen

Beetle

Insects

A typical insect is made up of three parts: head, thorax, and abdomen. It also has six legs, and most have two pairs of wings. On the head are eyes; mouthparts; and a pair of antennae, or feelers.

Other invertebrates

There are many other groups of invertebrates, including familiar creatures such as worms, snails, and crabs. There are also countless other species, many of which are invisible to the naked eye.

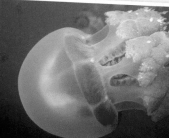

Cnidarian (jellyfish)

Echinoderm (sea urchin)

Spiders

Spiders are not insects but arachnids. This group of invertebrates also includes scorpions as well as tiny mites and ticks, and all have four pairs of legs.

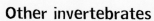

Spider

Crustacean (crab)

MAMMALS

Marsupials

Marsupial means "pouched mammal," and all female marsupials have a pouch, or some folds of skin on their body where their tiny young can feed, grow, and develop in safety. They stay in the pouch for several months. There are more than 300 kinds of marsupial. Most live in Australia and its surrounding islands, but there are some in South America and one species—the Virginia opossum—lives in North America.

Gilbert's potoroo is the world's rarest marsupial. There are only about 40 left in the wild.

Virginia opossum

Cuscus

Night creatures

Opossums and possums, such as the cuscus, usually sleep during the day and come out at night to find food. Possums feed mainly on leaves, but the Virginia opossum also eats small animals.

A strong tail acts as a fifth limb and support.

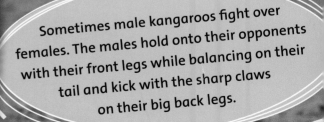

STRANGE DIET?

Eucalyptus leaves are poisonous to us, but the koala and two other kinds of marsupial—the greater glider and the ringtail possum—eat them all day long.

Fussy eater Koalas are very choosy. There are 500 kinds of eucalyptus trees, but the koala eats the leaves of only 35 of them.

Thirsty? Koalas hardly ever drink and get nearly all the liquid they need from their food.

Eucalyptus leaves

Koala

Sometimes male kangaroos fight over females. The males hold onto their opponents with their front legs while balancing on their tail and kick with the sharp claws on their big back legs.

DID YOU KNOW? The long-tailed planigale's body is only about 2 inches (6 centimeters) long.

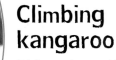

Climbing kangaroo

Did you know there are kangaroos that live in trees? The tree kangaroo spends nearly all its time high up in the trees, eating leaves and fruit.

Large ears can turn in all directions to pick up sounds.

A long tail helps the tree kangaroo to balance.

Huge back legs have powerful muscles.

Pademelon

Nail-tailed wallaby

Wallabies

The quokka, pademelons, and other wallabies belong to the same family as kangaroos, but they are much smaller. Like kangaroos, they bound along on their strong back legs and they eat plants. The nail-tailed wallaby gets its name from the nail-like point at the tip of its tail.

Quokka

INCREDIBLE JOURNEY

A two-day-old kangaroo baby weighs less than a sugar cube.

A female kangaroo stands nearly as tall as an adult human, but she gives birth to a baby the size of a jelly bean. The little creature must make its own way to its mother's pouch where it can feed and grow in safety.

This joey is eight months old and almost ready to leave its mother's pouch.

Speedy leaper

The red kangaroo is the largest marsupial and weighs up to 200 pounds (90 kilograms). It can leap along at 35 miles (56 kilometers) an hour and cover 30 feet (9 meters) in a single bound.

Marsupials

Bandicoot

Super burrower

The wombat looks rather like a little bear. It is an excellent digger and burrows into the ground with the help of its strong claws. It feeds mostly on plant matter, such as grass and roots.

Insect eaters

Termites are the favorite food of the numbat. It tears open the nest with its strong claws and then laps up the insects with its long tongue. Bandicoots also eat insects but prey on other small animals too and eat plants.

Numbat

Bone cruncher

The Tasmanian devil is the largest carnivorous marsupial and certainly the fiercest. It has amazingly powerful jaws and can crunch through the toughest skin and even the bones of its prey. It eats anything it can find, including carrion.

Meat eater

There are four kinds of quoll, all of which are carnivores that feed on animals such as lizards, birds, and insects. Quoll also eat carrion (dead animals) and plant matter.

The Tasmanian devil is a very noisy creature and makes a range of sounds, including deep growls and blood-curdling screeches.

DID YOU KNOW? The marsupial mole has no visible eyes or ears.

Deadly venom

The male platypus is one of the very few venomous mammals. It has a sharp spur on each hind foot that connects to a venom gland in its leg. The platypus uses its venom to defend itself against attackers.

A broad tail for steering in water

A sensitive rubbery beak for finding food

Webbed feet for swimming power

The platypus has five strong claws on each foot.

Monotremes

The echidna and the platypus are the only mammals that lay eggs instead of giving birth to live young. The females keep the eggs warm while they develop. When the young hatch, their mothers feed them milk, but the mothers do not have teats. The milk simply oozes from slits in the fur. The platypus, with its ducklike beak and tail like a beaver, is one of the most extraordinary of all animals. It hunts in water and eats shellfish, worms, and insect larvae.

Long-nosed echidna

ECHIDNAS

The long hard spines on the echidnas are the reason for their other common name—spiny anteaters.

Short nose The short-nosed echidna lives in New Guinea and Australia. It scurries around on the ground searching for insects and worms to eat.

Short-nosed echidna

Long nose The long-nosed echidna's snout can be up to 8 inches (20 cm) long. Scientists believe that an echidna's snout is highly sensitive and can pick up the tiny electrical signals given off by its prey. Echidnas also have a long sticky tongue for mopping up their prey.

Sloths and relatives

These strange creatures might look very different from one another, but they all have special joints in the lower part of their backbone that give them extra support and strength for burrowing or climbing. There are about 31 species, most of which have no teeth, and they all live in North, Central, and South America.

Tamandua

A sloth's fur grows the opposite way of that of other mammals. When the sloth is upside down the fur hangs down, and water can run off.

ANTEATERS

The four kinds of anteaters all have long snouts and strong claws for digging. Most have no teeth, but they can capture insects with their extra-long tongues.

Climber The tamandua, or lesser anteater, is a good climber and can break into insect nests in the trees as well as on the ground to find food. It lives in South America.

Big eater The giant anteater is up to 6 feet (2 m) long, including its tail, and is the largest of the family. It is said to eat up to 35,000 ants or termites a day! Its tongue is 2 feet (60 cm) long.

Giant anteater

Hanging around

Sloths spend nearly all their time hanging in the trees, feeding on leaves and buds. They come down to the ground only to defecate but cannot walk properly and have to drag themselves along with their front legs. However, sloths are good swimmers and move with ease in the water.

Armored armadillo

Armadillos are covered with an amazing series of bony plates that makes it very hard for predators to attack them. They feed mostly on insects, such as ants and termites, which they lap up with their long, sticky tongue.

The moonrat marks its territory with a scent said to smell like rotting onions!

Tenrec

Spiky

Moonrats and tenrecs both have coarse spiky fur, but the hedgehog's back and sides are covered with sharp spines, which protect it from predators. If attacked, the hedgehog can roll itself up into a prickly ball.

Insectivores

As their name suggests, these busy little creatures do mainly feed on insects, but they also hunt other creatures such as frogs and eat some plants. Most have rounded bodies, short legs, and long snouts. Their eyesight is generally poor, but they find prey with the help of their good sense of smell. Most live on land, but some, such as the web-footed tenrec and the water shrew, swim well.

Western European hedgehog

IN THE FAMILY?

Moles and golden moles may look the same, but they belong to different families.

Golden mole

Both kinds of moles have short, dense fur. They live in underground burrows, which they dig with their strong claws.

The European mole spends most of its life underground.

Shrews

There are many different kinds of shrews, but all are small and mouselike with long pointed noses. One of the world's smallest animals is a shrew—the pygmy shrew is so tiny it can crawl into earthworm tunnels.

DID YOU KNOW? Shrews are very active and need lots of food. They can eat their own body weight in a day.

Bats

Although some mammals can glide through the air, bats are the only ones that truly fly. A bat has wings made of skin, supported on long finger bones, and is agile and speedy in the air. Many bats eat insects while others prey on small animals, such as lizards. Others feed on fruit and on pollen and nectar from flowers. Most bats are active at night.

Insect eaters

The little pipistrelle is an insect-eating bat. It darts around at night, snatching and eating flies and other insects in the air. Flies are its main prey, and it may gobble up several thousand in one night.

The flying fox is a kind of fruit bat. Its wings measure up to 6 feet (1.8 m) from tip to tip.

Fruit eaters

Fruit bats are the largest bats. The bats spend the day hanging upside down in forest trees and fly out at night to search for ripe fruit and flower nectar to eat. Fruit bats have larger eyes and better sight than most bats.

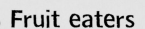

DID YOU KNOW? The hog-nosed bat is one of the world's smallest mammals.

BLOOD FEEDER

The vampire bat is the only mammal that feeds entirely on blood.

The vampire bat crawls up onto its victim, bites into the animal's flesh with razor-sharp teeth, and then laps up the blood that flows from the wound.

The vampire bat needs at least two tablespoons of blood a day.

The noctule bat flies at speeds of up to 30 miles (50 km) an hour.

Daubenton's bat feeds on fish as well as insects. It swoops close to the water surface and snatches fish with its feet.

SPECIAL SENSE

Some special features help bats with their powers of echolocation. Bats also have good senses of smell and hearing.

- **Large ears** These are important for picking up as much as possible from the echoes that bounce back from a bat's echolocating sounds.

- **Nose leaf** Many bats that use echolocation have a strangely shaped nose, made up of lots of folds of skin, called a nose leaf. This helps to direct the sounds more accurately.

The horseshoe bat has a very complex nose leaf.

Finding prey

Bats use echolocation—a type of sonar—to help them find prey in the dark. The bat shouts out a loud sound that is too high for us to hear. It then listens for the echoes that help it work out the size and position of objects, such as moths, in its path.

It's about the size of a bumblebee and weighs 0.05 to 0.07 ounces (1.4 to 2 grams).

Lemurs

Long-legged lemurs are primates like monkeys and apes, but they are more primitive and have smaller brains. Their group name is *prosimians*, which means "before apes." Lemurs live in Madagascar, but their relatives, including smaller creatures such as bush babies, lorises, and pottos, are found in Africa and parts of Southeast Asia. Most prosimians have long legs for jumping and climbing and shorter arms. There are about 85 species in all.

The greater bamboo lemur is the rarest of the lemurs, and there may be fewer than 100 of these animals left in the wild.

On the ground, the sifaka, a kind of lemur, leaps along upright on two legs.

Male ring-tailed lemurs rub smelly secretions onto their tail, then wave it around to attract females.

Galago

Leaping lemurs

Lemurs are amazingly athletic animals, both on the ground and up in the trees. All except the indri have a long tail that helps them balance as they leap between branches or bounce along on the ground. The tail cannot be used for grasping.

DID YOU KNOW? Bush babies, such as the galago, make a sound like a child crying.

NIGHT CREATURES

Many prosimians are mainly active at night and have large eyes to help them see in poor light. These two species both have hands that are adapted for their lifestyles.

Grasping hands The potto has stumpy little index fingers and opposable thumbs, making its hands ideal for grasping branches.

Fantastic finger The aye-aye has a very long middle finger on each hand that it uses to extract insects from little holes in tree bark.

Potto

The aye-aye's middle finger is two or three times longer than the rest of its fingers.

Each of a tarsier's eyes is as big as its brain.

Tiny climbers

Tarsiers live in rain forests in Southeast Asia. Tarsiers spend most of their time in the trees where they climb with ease as they catch insects to eat. They are small animals and only weigh up to 6 ounces (165 g)—not much more than an apple.

CUTE BUT DEADLY

The slow loris may look cuddly, but it has a nasty bite.

On the inside of the loris's elbows are special patches that store a poisonous substance. If in danger, the loris sucks up some poison and then delivers it to the enemy with a vicious bite.

The loris has extra-sharp teeth in its lower jaw.

Monkeys and apes

The great apes—gorillas, chimpanzees, bonobos, and orangutans—are our closest relatives in the animal kingdom, and they are highly intelligent, agile animals. Also in the primate group are the gibbons, or lesser apes, and monkeys. Most primates have thumbs that they can press against their fingers as we can, allowing them to grip well and handle small objects.

OLD WORLD MONKEYS

The 96 or so species of Old World monkeys live in Africa and Asia. The group includes baboons, guenons, and macaques.

Confident climber The colobus monkey spends most of its life in the treetops, where it feeds on leaves. Unlike other monkeys, it does not have thumbs.

Big monkeys Baboons are some of the largest of all monkeys. They live in Africa and the Middle East in large troops and hunt animals, such as young antelopes, as well as eat plants.

Colobus monkey

Gelada baboons

Gorillas might look big and fierce, but they eat only fruit and leaves and occasionally snack on insects.

Gentle giants

Gorillas are the largest of the great apes. They grow up to 6 feet (1.8 m) tall and weigh as much as 485 pounds (220 kg). They live in family groups of up to 30 animals, led by one or more adult males, and they spend most of the day feeding.

Hamadryas baboon

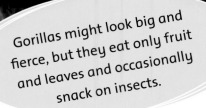

A gibbon can leap an incredible 30 feet (9 m) in a single bound.

Forest apes

Orangutans are now rare and live only on the islands of Sumatra and Borneo. They are good climbers and spend most of their lives high in rain forest trees, feeding on fruit. They live alone, except for mothers and then young.

Amazing acrobats

Gibbons are the most acrobatic of all the primates. They travel through the treetops at a high speed, swinging from branch to branch on their long arms. There are 11 species of gibbon, and all live in Southeast Asia.

A gibbon's arms are longer than its legs!

CLEVER CHIMPS

Chimpanzees are among the few animals that use tools.

Chimps "fish" for termites. The chimp wiggles a stick into a hole in a termite nest. The termites attack the intruding stick. Then the chimp pulls it up and eats the insects.

New World monkeys

The red howler monkey and the golden lion tamarin are two of the 75 or so species of New World monkeys living in the forests of Central and South America. Nearly all have a long tail, and in some, the tail is prehensile and can be used like a fifth limb for gripping.

Golden lion tamarin

Red howler monkey

DID YOU KNOW? The howler monkey's loud whooping call can be heard from nearly 3 miles (5 km) away!

Caring parents

Most mammals take good care of their families. A mother feeds her young on milk from her own body, and many mammals keep their babies with them for long periods, defending them from danger and teaching them how to survive on their own. Big cat cubs, for example, need to learn how to hunt by watching their mother for many months before trying to make their own kills. Smaller creatures must learn how to hide from predators.

A young animal is vulnerable, and parents must always be on the lookout for danger.

A cheetah defends her cubs fiercely.

Lots to learn

A mother chimpanzee must teach her baby many things, such as which plants and other foods are good to eat—and which are not— where to find water, and how to build nests in the trees for sleeping. A young chimp stays with its mother for three or four years or more.

A baby elephant drinks at least 3 gallons (11.4 liters) of its mother's milk every day.

Dogs

Wild dogs are fast-running predators that chase their victims for long distances before attacking with their strong jaws and sharp teeth. They have excellent senses, particularly of smell. There are about 36 species, including wolves, foxes, and coyotes, and they live all over the world. Domestic dogs are descended from wolves. Some dogs, such as wolves, move in close-knit groups called packs, but others, including foxes, live and hunt alone.

COLOR CHANGE

The arctic fox changes its coat with the seasons.

In the winter, the arctic fox's snow-white coat helps it stay hidden from enemies and prey. In the summer when the snow melts, its fur turns brownish gray to blend with the tundra plants.

Summer coat

Winter coat

Pack life

Gray wolves are the largest of the dog family and can measure up to 5 feet (1.5 m) long with a 20-inch (50 cm) tail. A wolf pack contains up to 12 animals, led by a dominant male and female pair. The pack hunts together.

All pack members help to feed and care for the young.

Bush dogs

The stocky little bush dog of South American forests has shorter legs than most dogs. It hunts large rodents but can also swim well and catches prey in water.

DID YOU KNOW? The dhole (right) makes a strange whistling call to keep in touch with its pack.

OPPORTUNISTS

Some dogs are not only good hunters but also take any food they can find, including other hunters' leftovers.

Scavengers Coyotes are fast-moving predators, but they are not above foraging for food in rubbish as well as eating carrion—animals that are already dead.

Food thieves Jackals will eat dead animals and snatch what they can from the kills of other animals, such as lions. Jackals also eat fruit and berries.

A jackal carrying off a dead flamingo.

In most packs, only the dominant male and female mate and bear young.

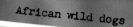
African wild dogs

Strength in numbers

African wild dogs live in packs and are very well-organized hunters. Together, they can bring down animals much larger than themselves, such as zebra and wildebeest. The dogs have great stamina and will pursue prey for miles. Dingos also often hunt in packs.

Dingos fighting over a kill

Bears

Although bears are the largest flesh-eating land mammals, most feed more on plants and insects than larger prey. Only the polar bear hunts for the bulk of its food. Typically, a bear has a big, strong body; powerful legs; and a short tail. There are eight species, including the panda, which used to be thought of as part of the raccoon family.

The giant panda is the world's rarest bear. There are probably only about 2,500 left in the wild.

Polar bears are excellent swimmers and can swim 100 miles (160 km) or more. The paws are partially webbed.

A brown bear's claws can be more than 4 inches (10 cm) long.

Arctic master

The mighty polar bear is the largest of all the bears and the fiercest. It hunts on land and in water and feeds mostly on seals. The polar bear has good sight and hearing and can also sniff out prey from more than 19 miles (30 km) away.

Speedy giant

Brown bears are the most widespread of all bears and live in North America, Europe, and Asia. They grow up to 8 feet (2.5 m) long and weigh as much as 700 pounds (318 kg)—more than four people. They run surprisingly fast at up to 30 miles (48 km) an hour.

American black bear

TROPICAL BEARS

Not all bears live in cold places. Two of the smallest members of the bear family live in tropical rain forests.

Spectacled bear This is the only bear in South America. It gets its name from the markings around its eyes, and these markings are slightly different on each bear!

. . . .

Smallest bear The little sun bear lives in rain forests in Southeast Asia and is a good tree climber. It's also called the honey bear because it loves to eat honey.

Spectacled bear

Sun bear

The sun bear laps up insects with its 10-inch (25 cm) tongue.

Asiatic black bear

Black bears

There are two kinds of black bear: the Asiatic and the American black bear. Both feed mainly on plants, nuts, and berries, but they will gobble up insects and other small animals too. Asiatic bears also eat carrion.

BAMBOO BEAR

The giant panda feeds almost entirely on bamboo.

The panda spends most of its time eating, consuming 44 pounds (20 kg) of bamboo a day. Strong jaws and teeth help the panda crush its tough food, and it has an extra "thumb" on each hand to help it grip the stems.

DID YOU KNOW? A newborn giant panda weighs only as much as an apple.

Small carnivores

Despite their size, these relatives of dogs and cats are very skillful predators. Mustelids, such as stoats and otters, have long bodies, short legs, and a keen sense of smell for tracking down prey. The civets, which include meerkats and genets, are more catlike. Most are hunters, but a few, such as the palm civet, eat only plants. The four species of hyenas might look like dogs but, in fact, are more closely related to civets.

Standing guard

Meerkats are a kind of mongoose. They live in close-knit family groups of up to 40 or so animals, and they share the work of finding food and watching out for danger.

Meerkats make more than 20 sounds, each of which has a different meaning.

EXPERT HUNTERS

Most mustelids and civets are agile, aggressive creatures with sharp teeth and claws.

Speedy killers Agile little stoats are fast runners and powerful killers. A stoat can pursue an animal such as a rabbit, which is ten times its size, until it gives up and then kill it with a speedy bite to the neck.

Big biters Wolverines are relatives of stoats but much larger. They have incredibly powerful jaws and can bite through frozen flesh and attack animals as big as caribou.

Smelly warning Genets are good climbers and hunt birds and other animals up in the trees as well as on the ground. Like skunks, the genet can squirt out a nasty-smelling liquid to warn off attackers.

Stoat

Wolverine

Genet

Meerkats build complex burrows with tunnels and sleeping chambers, where they shelter at night.

TEAMWORK

The honey badger has a helper in its search for food.

Honeyguide

It watches out for a bird called the honeyguide. When the bird finds a bees' nest, it makes a special call. The badger follows the bird and breaks open the nest with its strong claws. While the badger feasts on honey and bee larvae, the honeyguide eats wax as well as larvae.

Honey badger

Power jaws

The spotted hyena has amazingly strong jaws and can crunch through tough skin and even bones, which its powerful digestive system can break down. The hyena does scavenge from other predators, but it is also a skillful hunter.

Super stinky

If in danger, the striped skunk has a special way of defending itself. It turns its back on its enemy, lifts its tail, and squirts out a very nasty-smelling fluid. The fluid burns the attacker's eyes and nose, and the attacker learns to stay well clear!

Tool user

The sea otter is one of the few animals that uses tools to help it feed. Having found a clam or other shellfish, the otter lies on its back with a rock on its chest. It bangs the clam on the rock until the shell breaks and the otter can eat the juicy flesh.

DID YOU KNOW? The sea otter's fur contains approximately 800 million hairs!

The Iberian lynx is the world's most endangered wild cat. There are fewer than 200 adult animals left in the wild.

Cats

Cats, from the mighty tiger to the little wild cat, are all superb predators and amazingly similar in their structure. There are about 38 species found all over the world except Australia and Antarctica. Cats have a strong supple body, sharp teeth and claws, and excellent senses to help them find their prey. Many have striped or spotted coats that help them blend in with the surroundings and creep up on their prey.

World beater

The cheetah is the fastest land animal over short distances. It can run at more than 60 miles (100 km) an hour—but only for up to a minute. Its flexible spine helps it move fast, and its long tail aids balance.

Lionesses hunt together and can bring down prey as large as buffalo.

Big cat family

Lions are the only cats that live in groups. Related females and their young live together in a group called a pride in the territory defended by one or more males. Females suckle one another's young.

Lions are one of only four kinds of cats that can roar. The others are tigers, leopards, and jaguars.

DID YOU KNOW? The snow leopard sometimes uses its furry tail like a scarf to keep itself warm.

SMALL CATS

About three-quarters of cat species are less than 3 feet (1 m) long—not much larger than a domestic pet cat.

Iberian lynx This rare cat lives in Spain and preys mostly on rabbits. Lynx are being bred in captivity for release into the wild to try and increase the population.

Black-footed cat One of the smallest of all wild cats, this species preys on small prey such as insects and mice.

Ocelot This spotted cat lives in South American rain forests and is an expert climber. Its markings help it hide in the dappled light and shade of the forest.

Iberian lynx

Ocelot

Biggest big cat

Tigers are the largest cats, and the Siberian tigers are the biggest of all. They are more than 10 feet (3 m) long and weigh up to 660 pounds (300 kg)—as much as four humans. They hunt prey such as deer and wild boar.

SNOW CAT

Not all cats live in jungles . . .

The snow leopard lives on high mountains in central Asia and has thick fur and even furry feet to keep it warm. It is amazingly athletic and is said to make the longest jump by a cat—50 feet (15 m). The human long jump record is 29 feet (8.95 m).

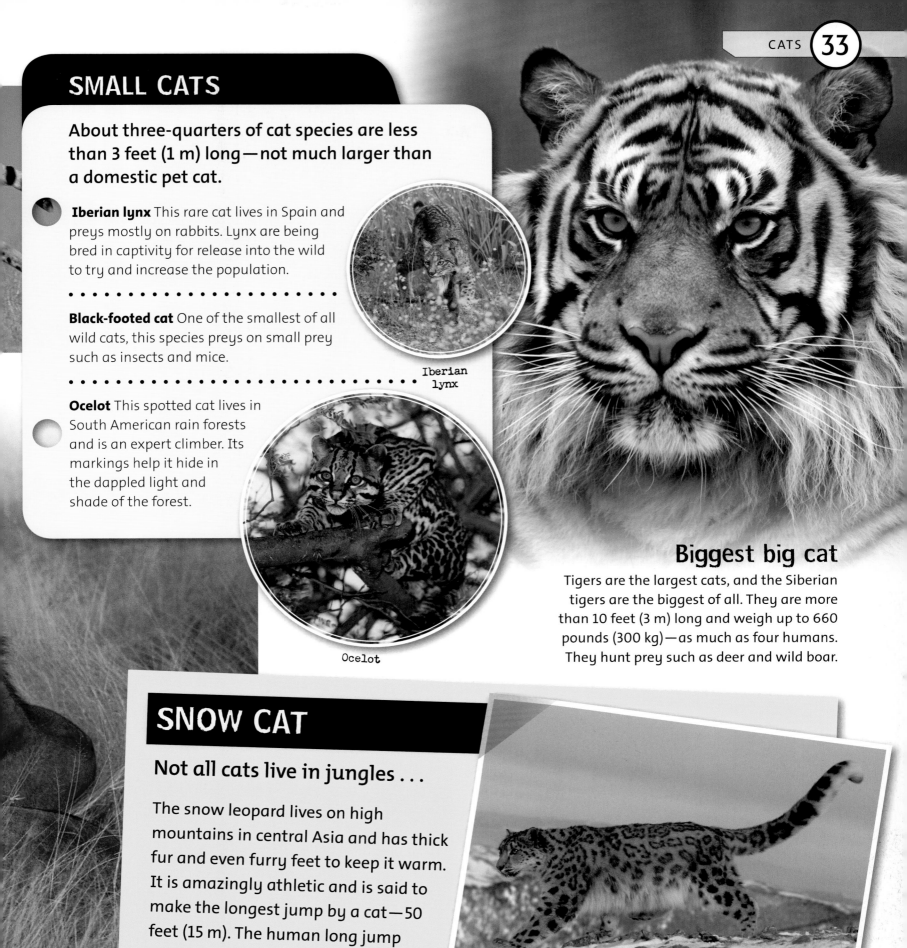

Seals and sea lions

Sleek and streamlined with flippers instead of legs, seals and sea lions swim and dive with ease. They are mammals and closely related to cats and dogs, but they spend most of their time in water and only come to land to bask in the sun or to give birth to their babies. There are about 35 species of seals and sea lions and one species of walrus. They live all over the world, mostly in the sea, although there are some freshwater seals.

Freshwater seals

Baikal seals are the smallest seals and the only ones that spend their whole life in freshwater. The seals' home is Lake Baikal in Asia, which is the world's deepest lake and covered with ice for five months of the year. The seals give birth to their pups in dens made on the ice.

AWESOME WHISKERS

Sensitive whiskers help seals and sea lions find prey.

All seals and sea lions have whiskers. These pick up vibrations in the water and help the animals find prey, particularly where visibility is low such as below ice floes. The whiskers also seem to help seals find their way underwater.

A fur seal's whiskers can grow to 20 inches (50 cm) long.

The walrus's long tusks are actually giant teeth and can be up to 3 feet (1 m) long!

Both male and female walruses have tusks—those of females are usually longer.

FINDING FOOD

Seals find all their food in the water, and they are skilled hunters.

Strange teeth The crabeater seal feeds more on shrimplike krill than crabs. It sifts krill from the water through its special teeth, which fit together like a strainer.

Fierce predator The leopard seal is the most predatory of all seals and catches fish, squid, and penguins with its long, sharp teeth. It is the only seal that also preys on other seals.

The leopard seal gets its name from its spotty markings—and its fierce habits.

Mating call

The southern elephant seal is the largest of the seals. A male can be up to 20 feet (6 m) long—longer than an average car—and weigh almost 4.5 tons (4 metric tons). The male has a long trunklike snout, which he inflates when roaring at rivals in the mating season.

A thick layer of fatty blubber under the skin helps keep the walrus warm in Arctic waters.

Fast swimmer

The California sea lion is one of the fastest swimming pinnipeds and can move through the water at up to 25 miles (40 km) an hour. It is an expert diver too and slows its heart rate when diving so it can stay underwater for longer. Like all sea lions, it has little ear flaps. Seals have small ear openings but no external flaps.

Giant tusks

The walrus uses its long tusks to haul itself up onto ice floes and to chop breathing holes in the ice. It also uses them to defend itself and its young against attacks by other animals.

DID YOU KNOW? Only sea lions can tuck their back flippers under them to move on land.

Whales

The largest of all animals, whales are mammals, but they spend their whole lives in water. Their bodies are beautifully streamlined for swimming, and they have flippers instead of legs. Unlike seals and sea lions, whales do not come to land to give birth—their young are born in the water. There are two sorts of whales. Baleen whales, such as the humpback and the blue whale, feed by filtering tiny creatures from the water; toothed whales, which include dolphins and porpoises, hunt and capture larger prey.

A humpback calf is up to 14.7 feet (4.5 m) long at birth.

Krill

Filter feeders

The huge humpback whale feeds on krill and small fish, which it filters from the water through its baleen plates. It eats as much as 1.4 ton (1.300 metric tons) of food a day. The female gives birth to one calf every two or three years and feeds her young on her rich milk for a year.

DOLPHINS

Dolphins are small, toothed whales. Most live in the sea, but there are a few freshwater dolphins.

Jungle dolphin The Amazon river dolphin lives in the murky waters of the Amazon and has long beaklike jaws for finding food in the muddy riverbed.

Common dolphin These fast-swimming dolphins often swim in groups of more than a thousand, making spectacular leaps above the waves as they speed along.

Deep diver

The northern bottlenose is a toothed whale and hunts prey such as fish and squid. When searching for food, it makes deep dives, lasting an hour or more, and has been known to go down to depths of 4,700 feet (1,450 m). The bottlenose grows to about 30 feet (9 m) long and weighs up to 8.3 tons (7.5 metric tons).

Common dolphin

Amazon river dolphin

Northern bottlenose whale

An adult humpback is up to 50 feet (15 m) long and can weigh 44 tons (40 metric tons).

The humpback whale has up to 400 fringed baleen plates hanging from each side of its upper jaw.

Humpback whales communicate with one another in complex songs that last about 20 minutes and are repeated for hours.

BIGGEST EVER

At 98 feet (30 m) long, the blue whale is the biggest animal that has ever lived.

Even a newborn baby blue whale is 23 feet (7 m) long, longer than a car, and it drinks the equivalent of a bathtub of milk every day.

An adult blue whale eats 6.5 tons (6 metric tons) of krill a day.

Top predators

The killer whale, or orca, is a superb hunter and even comes almost onto the shore to capture prey such as seals. Killer whales live in family groups, called pods, and hunt together, capturing other whales and even great white sharks.

DID YOU KNOW? The blue whale's tongue weighs as much as an elephant!

Elephants

The mighty African bush elephant is the largest of all land mammals, weighing in at more than 7.5 tons (7 metric tons). There are two other species of elephant—the forest elephant, which also lives in Africa, and the Asian elephant. All live in close-knit family groups of females and their young, led by the oldest female. Males live alone or in groups of other males and join the females only for mating. Elephants feed on plant matter, such as leaves, grass, and bark.

Mother and calf

A young Asian elephant is on its feet soon after birth. It feeds on its mother's milk at first but starts to eat grass and other plants at a few months old. It stays close to its mother for at least three or four years, and all its "aunties" in the herd help to care for it too.

ELE-FACTS

All elephants have big ears and a very sensitive trunk.

Asian elephant The ears of the Asian elephant are smaller than those of its African relatives, and it has one "finger" at the end of its trunk. Its back is slightly humped. Males generally have tusks, but most females do not.

African bush elephant This species has very large ears and two "fingers" at the end of its trunk. Males and females have tusks.

African forest elephant Smaller than the bush elephant, this animal has straighter tusks. Its skin is darker, and its ears are a more rounded shape.

Forest elephant

African elephant

Hyraxes, sea cows, and aardvarks

Hyraxes are often said to be the elephants' closest relatives, but this is not strictly true. They do, however, share a common ancestor with elephants and sea cows, and despite their very different appearances, there are some similarities in the bones and teeth of all these animals. The aardvark is a rarely seen, nocturnal insect eater and the only member of its family.

The aardvark feasts on as many as 100,000 ants and termites a night.

Master diggers

The aardvark lives in Africa and is a powerful digger. It feeds only on ants and termites and uses its strong feet and claws to tear apart the insects' nests. It laps up its prey with its sticky tongue, which can be up to 1 foot (30 cm) long.

Sea cows

Sirenians, or sea cows, are the only plant-eating aquatic mammals. These bulky, slow-moving creatures spend their whole lives in water but, like whales, must come to the surface to breathe. There are four species—the dugong and three kinds of manatee— and all are now rare.

Dugong

West Indian manatee

FEET FOR CLIMBING

Hyraxes, which look like large guinea pigs, are expert climbers.

A hyrax's feet look like little hooves, but they have rubbery soles that are kept moist by special glands. The soles act like suction pads and provide a powerful grip as the hyrax climbs on rocks and trees.

Hyraxes live in family groups led by a dominant male.

DID YOU KNOW? When the manatee's teeth wear down, they are replaced with new ones.

Rhinos, tapirs, and horses

The feature that links the animals in these three families is that they all have an odd number of toes. Horses have just one toe, while rhinoceroses and tapirs have three. Horses, including asses and zebras, are fast, graceful animals with long, slender legs. Rhinos are huge bulky creatures, and all weigh more than a ton (0.9 metric tons). Tapirs are smaller and piglike and live in tropical forests.

Rhinos in danger

There are five species of rhinoceros, and all but the white rhino are in serious danger of becoming extinct. Thanks to conservation efforts, numbers of white rhinos have increased, and there are now more of this species than all the other kinds put together.

Black rhinoceros

A rhino's horns are made of keratin, the same substance as our hair and fingernails.

NO TWO THE SAME!

There are three species of zebra, and all have a different stripe pattern.

In fact, no two zebras have exactly the same arrangement of stripes. All are slightly different, and even the left and right sides of an animal aren't exactly the same!

Przewalski's horse

Wild horses

Przewalski's horse is the only surviving ancestor of domestic horses. It became extinct in the wild, but it has since been bred in captivity and reintroduced in Mongolia, its original home. The onager is a fast-running wild ass and has been timed at 43 miles (70 km) an hour.

Burchell's zebras at a waterhole

Onager mot
and foal

DID YOU KNOW? The zebra has amazing eyesight, and its night vision is as good as an owl

The Sumatran is the smallest of the rhinos, and there are probably fewer than 200 left in the wild.

RHINO RELATIONS

There are four kinds of tapir. Three live in South America and the fourth in Asia. All are now becoming rare.

Living on land and in water The biggest tapirs are the size of large pigs, but they are fast runners and good swimmers. They feed on plants on land and in water.

Stripy babies Baby tapirs have rows of white spots and stripes along their backs. Tapirs live in forests, and these markings help break up the body outline and keep the vulnerable babies hidden from predators.

The white markings disappear as the baby grows up.

There are now more than 20,000 white rhinos in Africa.

Armored rhino

The Indian, or one-horned rhino, has a particularly well-protected body. The skin is about 1 inch (2.5 cm) thick on the back and sides and arranged in sections, making it look like a suit of armor.

African wild ass

⚠ There are thought to be only 200 African wild asses left in the wild!

Hippos, deer, and relatives

Animals as different as tiny chevrotain, huge hippopotamuses, and the towering giraffes all belong to a group called Artiodactyla, or even-toed hoofed mammals. Most are plant eaters, but wild pigs eat more or less anything, including other animals. There are only a few species of camels, giraffes, and hippos, but there are 44 different kinds of deer. Nearly all male deer have large branching antlers, and both male and female caribou have antlers.

Hippos swim well and can also run along the riverbed.

Heavyweight hippo

The hippopotamus is one of the heaviest land animals, after rhinos and elephants, and weighs up to 1.5 tons (1.4 metric tons). It spends much of its day in water to stay cool and avoid sunburn. At night it comes to land to feed on grass.

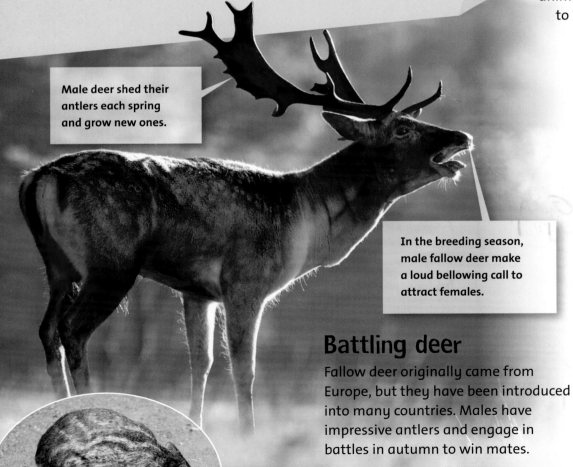

Male deer shed their antlers each spring and grow new ones.

In the breeding season, male fallow deer make a loud bellowing call to attract females.

Battling deer

Fallow deer originally came from Europe, but they have been introduced into many countries. Males have impressive antlers and engage in battles in autumn to win mates.

Powerful pigs

Wild boars live in Europe, Asia, and North Africa and are the most widespread of the 14 or so kinds of wild pigs. Wild boars are powerful, fast-moving creatures and feed on more or less anything they can find. Males have sharp tusks.

<u>DID YOU KNOW?</u> Chevrotain are the smallest deer, just 1 foot (30 cm) to the shoulder!

TRICKY CONDITIONS

Animals in the camel family, which includes guanacos and vicuñas, have to adapt to some difficult living conditions.

Mountain dweller The guanaco lives in the Andes Mountains at altitudes of up to 13,000 feet (4,000 m). It has more red blood cells than other animals, and this helps it cope well with the low oxygen levels in its mountain home.

Desert life The camel can store fat in its humps, which helps it survive in times of poor food supplies. It can go without water for several weeks.

Guanaco

The giraffe has seven neck bones, just like we do, but each one is very long.

Bactrian camel

The Bactrian's thick coat keeps it warm in the cold Gobi Desert winter.

Giraffe

LONGEST TONGUES

Giraffes and their relatives okapis have extra-long tongues.

The okapi's tongue measures about 1 foot (30 cm) and is so long the animal can lick its own eyelids. The giraffe's tongue is even longer at up to 18 inches (46 cm)—almost as long as your arm!

Okapi

Standing tall

The giraffe is the world's tallest mammal at nearly 20 feet (6 m). Even a newborn baby giraffe is 6 feet (2 m)—taller than an adult human. Acacia trees are the giraffe's main food, and it manages to gather the leaves with its long tongue, despite the sharp thorns.

Wild cattle and relatives

The biggest group of even-toed hoofed mammals includes cattle and their relatives: sheep, goats, and antelopes. There are over 140 species, more than half of which live in Africa. Most are large animals, and all the males, as well as some females, have unbranched horns that are never shed. These are plant-eating animals and are the favorite food of many predators. They have keen senses of sight, hearing, and smell to help them avoid their hunters.

Thomson's gazelle

ANTELOPES

Antelopes are fast-running animals that live in Africa and parts of Asia.

Agile gazelle One of the most common gazelles in Africa, the Thomson's gazelle, makes bouncing movements—called stotting—as it runs. This tells predators that it is an agile animal and not worth pursuing.

Desert antelope The gemsbok can survive in dry areas with little water and gets much of the moisture it needs from its food, such as roots and melons. Males fight to win dominance of the herd.

Forest dweller Duikers are small antelopes that live in rain forests. They tend to hide in undergrowth rather than run when in danger.

Gemsbok

Spongy, rubbery hooves give bighorn sheep a good grip.

Dangerous journeys

Wildebeest are large antelope that live on grasslands in Africa. Every year, huge herds of thousands of wildebeest make long perilous migrations to follow the rains and find fresh grass to feed on.

LONG-DISTANCE CHAMPION

The pronghorn looks like an antelope but is actually in a family all of its own.

Although the pronghorn is not quite as speedy as the cheetah, it is the fastest-running mammal over long distances. This North American animal can run at over 30 miles (50 km) an hour for about 4 miles (6 km).

Agile climbers

Wild goats and sheep, such as the bighorn, usually live in mountainous areas and are expert climbers. Bighorn males have particularly large curling horns that they use in fights to win mates in the breeding season.

Surviving cold

Muskoxen *(right)* and yaks live in harsh climates, the muskoxen in temperatures of −40°F (−40°C) in the Arctic and the yak high in the Himalayas. Both have a double-layer coat—soft underfur to keep them warm and a top coat of long coarse hair for extra insulation.

Yak

DID YOU KNOW? Yaks live at more than 20,000 feet (6,000 m) in the Himalayas.

Rodents and rabbits

Rats, mice, and other rodents live all over the world, except in Antarctica, in habitats from desert and rain forests to Arctic tundra. All have large front teeth for gnawing food such as fruit, seeds, leaves, and, in a few cases, other animals, and these teeth continue to grow throughout life. With more than 2,000 species, rodents are the largest group of mammals and one of the most successful. Rabbits are a much smaller group with about 80 species.

Beavers often build dams of 130 feet (40 m) or more in length, but the largest so far recorded is an amazing 2,800 feet (850 m) long.

CAN SQUIRRELS FLY?

They cannot fly properly like bats, but they can glide from tree to tree.

Flying squirrels live in forests, and gliding is an efficient way of moving from tree to tree without going down to the ground. As the squirrel leaps, it spreads the loose flaps of skin at its sides; they then act like a parachute.

Flying squirrels can glide as far as 1,300 feet (400 m) from one branch to another.

Dam builders

Beavers probably have more effect on the area where they live than any animal other than humans. They cut down trees and branches with their strong teeth and use them to dam streams and create quiet ponds where they can live and build a lodge for shelter. Beavers feed on twigs, leaves, bark, and roots.

The capybara weighs up to 145 pounds (66 kg)— as much as a human.

Burrowing rodents

Prairie dogs are large rodents, not dogs. They live in colonies made up of lots of family groups and dig huge burrows that extend over a wide area and contain many chambers and tunnels. There are separate chambers for sleeping and caring for their young and even special toilet areas.

RATS AND MICE

With more than 1,000 species, this is the largest group of rodents.

Adaptable animals The secret of their success is their adaptability. Rats and mice can live in many different conditions and eat almost any kind of food, including scraps from our meals.

· ·

Pests Brown rats probably came from Asia originally but have now spread all over the world. They are now a serious pest and often spoil stored food supplies such as grain.

Brown rats can produce as many as 200 young in a year.

Prickly defense

Few predators dare to attack the porcupine with its coat of sharp quills. If an attacker does get too close, it may be pierced by the quills, which then detach from the porcupine.

Quills are up to 3 inches (8 cm) long.

European rabbit

North American pika

Biggest rodent

Capybaras live in South America and are the largest, heaviest rodents in the world. These heavily built, piglike animals are good swimmers and spend much of their time in water, feeding on water plants and other vegetation.

Rabbits, hares, and pikas

There are 80 or more species of rabbits, hares, and pikas. All feed on grass and other plants. Rabbits and hares are found all over the world and are fast-running animals with large ears and eyes. Pikas are smaller and look more like guinea pigs. They live in parts of Asia and North America.

DID YOU KNOW? The naked mole rat lives underground in a colony ruled by one female who bears all the young.

BIRDS

Flightless birds

Long-legged and speedy, the ostriches and their relatives are unable to fly, although they do have small wings. They rely on fast running, rather than flight, to escape from danger. This group of birds, also known as ratites, includes emus, rheas, and cassowaries, which are some of the largest of all birds, as well as kiwis, which are much smaller and have long beaks.

> The ostrich can run at least twice as fast as humans and can keep going for long distances.

40 mph/65 kph

FAMILY MATTERS

Ratites have some unusual breeding habits—the males do most of the work.

Emus and cassowaries Once a female emu has mated and laid her eggs, she leaves the male to incubate them, while she goes off and mates again. The male takes care of the young for up to two years. The cassowary male also incubates eggs and looks after his chicks.

Dominant pair Ostriches live in groups led by a dominant male and female. The male mates with several females in the group, and all the eggs are laid in the nest of the dominant female. She and her mate incubate all the eggs.

Emu chick

Cassowary

Big and fast

The ostrich is an extraordinary creature. As well as being the fastest-running bird, it is also the biggest. At about 6 feet (2 m) tall, it is taller than most people, and it weighs up to 350 pounds (160 kg). The ostrich also lays the biggest egg of any bird. Just one weighs about 4 pounds (1.75 kg)—about the same as 25 hens' eggs.

Sniffing for food

Like other ratites, the kiwi cannot fly. It spends its life on the ground, where it sniffs out food such as insects and fruit with the nostrils at the end of its beak. There are five species of kiwi, and all are now very rare.

DID YOU KNOW? The ostrich has the largest eyes of any land animal—up to 2 inches (5 cm) across!

Game birds

Pheasants, turkeys, grouse, and other game birds can fly, but they spend most of their lives on the ground. They scratch around for seeds, berries, and other food and snatch tasty morsels with their strong beaks. Game birds generally make their nests on the ground. Their chicks can run around a short time after hatching and are soon ready to leave the nest and start finding their own food. These birds are known as game birds because many kinds are hunted for food and for sport.

Sage grouse displaying to females

Attracting a mate

Game birds have a range of interesting ways of attracting mates. The peacock spreads his amazing tail feathers and struts back and forth to impress females. Male sage grouse display in groups. The birds puff up patches on their breast, spread their tails, and march around making special grunting sounds. The curassow relies on its voice and makes loud booming calls to attract females.

The yellow knob on the male curassow's beak gets bigger in the breeding season.

JUNGLE ANCESTOR

Our familiar domestic hens are descendants of the jungle fowl.

The brightly colored male red jungle fowl leads a flock of several females, which he defends from rival males, engaging in fierce fights if necessary. The female is much plainer with brownish-gold plumage.

The red jungle fowl lives in Southeast Asian rain forests.

Eyelike markings adorn the peacock's feathers.

Penguins

The most skillful swimmers and divers in the bird world are the penguins. They cannot fly, but in water, they use their flipperlike wings to push themselves along, and their sleek streamlined shape helps them move fast. There are about 17 species of penguins, many of which live in or around Antarctica.

There are more than 2 million king penguins in Antarctica, and a colony may contain hundreds of thousands of birds.

Life in a colony

King penguins gather in huge colonies on islands to mate and lay their eggs. When the chicks are old enough, their parents leave them together while they go to find food. Amazingly, the parents can recognize their own chick's call among the thousands of young shrieking for food.

Speedy swimmers

The gentoo penguin (above) is the fastest penguin in water and can swim at up to 22 miles (36 km) an hour. The Galápagos penguin is a speedy swimmer too. It lives farther north than any other penguin—its home is the Galápagos Islands, just north of the equator.

Galápagos penguin

Little penguin

DEVOTED FATHER

The emperor penguin incubates its egg during the Antarctic winter.

Once the female has laid her egg, her mate carries it on his feet to keep it warm through the icy weather. He cannot leave the egg or it would freeze, so he has to go without food for as long as 120 days.

Once the chick has hatched, the male holds it on his feet to keep it warm.

DID YOU KNOW? The little penguin weighs just 2 pounds (1 kg)—tiny compared to the 80 pound (37 kg) emperor penguin.

Divers and relatives

Although these birds belong to different groups, they all spend most of their lives in and around water. Albatrosses, shearwaters, and petrels can soar for hours over the ocean, swooping down to seize prey from surface waters. Divers and grebes live mostly around rivers and lakes, although divers are also seen in coastal areas.

LIFE ON THE WING

Shearwaters and petrels are fast, acrobatic flyers and also good swimmers, but they rarely come to land.

Surface feeder The storm petrel has a very special feeding technique. It swoops down to the sea and bounces along, its feet just pattering over the surface, as it searches for food.

Colony nesters The Manx shearwater only comes to land to breed. Huge colonies of birds nest on tiny islands and rocks.

Manx shearwater

Tubenoses Albatrosses, shearwaters, and petrels are also known as tubenoses because of the tubelike nostrils they have at the top of the beak.

Water bird

Features such as webbed feet and a streamlined body make the red-throated diver *(above)* an excellent swimmer. But these birds find it almost impossible to walk on land.

Wingspan 11 feet (3.5 m)

Longest wings

The wandering albatross has the longest wings of any bird. They measure an incredible 11 feet (3.5 m) from tip to tip. These birds fly thousands of kilometers across the sea in search of food for themselves and their young.

Courtship

Great crested grebes perform amazing courtship displays. The male and female bob their heads, spread their wings, and raise their crests in a kind of dance.

Pelicans, herons, and relatives

Ranging from predatory gannets to filter-feeding flamingos, the birds in these groups all live in and around water. Pelicans, cormorants, gannets, and frigatebirds are seabirds and have large feet with webbing between all four toes to help them swim. Herons, ibises, and flamingos usually live around freshwater. Their long legs allow them to wade into shallow water where they find food.

FLYING PIRATES

Frigatebirds soar over tropical areas of the Indian, Pacific, and Atlantic oceans.

Finding food The frigatebird watches for prey from the air, then swoops down to snatch it from the surface. It also feeds by attacking other seabirds and forcing them to give up their prey.

Great frigatebird

Attracting mates In the breeding season, the male frigatebird puffs up his scarlet throat pouch while calling to females.

Male frigatebird with inflated throat pouch

Fishing net

Under the pelican's long beak is a pouch of skin that the bird uses like a fishing net for gathering food. It scoops up a mouthful of fish and water, then brings its head up. The water escapes at the sides of the beak, and the bird swallows any fish whole.

Expert predator

The gannet catches its food in high-speed dives. It flies about 98 feet (30 m) above the surface watching for fish, then plunges into the sea like a flying harpoon to seize its prey.

The Australian pelican has the longest beak of any bird. It is up to 18 inches (47 cm)—about the length of an adult person's arm.

FILTER FEEDER

The long-legged flamingo's beak acts like a strainer to sift food from the water.

The bird wades into the shallows and bends down to place its beak under the surface. It takes in water and pushes it out through bristles at the sides of the beak with its large tongue. Any food is caught on these bristles and swallowed.

The flamingo holds its large beak upside down as it feeds.

Feeling for food

Ibises look very much like herons, but they feed in a very different way. The ibis hunts by touch, gently probing mud with its long, sensitive beak to find food such as crabs and other shellfish. The scarlet ibis flies up into trees to roost at night.

Daggerlike beak

Long-legged herons, such as the great blue heron (*above*), wade through shallow water, watching for fish or other prey, then seize it with a swift lunge of their long beak. Herons make nests of sticks in trees or on the ground. Both parents care for the eggs and their young.

DID YOU KNOW? The gannet can reach speeds of 60 miles (95 km) an hour as it dives!

Waterfowl and shorebirds

Ducks, geese, and swans—waterfowl—are plump, medium to large birds with webbed feet. They live in or around water. They usually feed in water and eat plants, fish, and other small creatures. All have young that hatch with a full coat of fluffy down feathers and can move about and find their own food almost immediately. Shorebirds are a very varied group of birds, which includes plovers, oystercatchers, and puffins as well as gulls and terns. Most shorebirds live around water and feed on aquatic creatures.

Fabulous feathers

The male mandarin duck is one of the most beautiful of all birds and uses the sail-like feathers on its sides in courtship displays to attract a mate. Mandarins nest in a tree. Soon after the chicks hatch, their mother calls them from the ground and they leap out of the nest.

Arctic terns make a round-trip of more than 43,500 miles (70,000 km) on their annual pole-to-pole migration.

WALKING ON WATER

Jacanas, also known as lily-trotters, have longer toes than any other bird.

Jacanas live in ponds and swamps. A jacana's extra-long toes help to spread its weight over a large area. This allows the bird to walk over floating lily pads as it searches for food such as insects and small water creatures.

The jacana's toes are about 5.5 inches (14 cm) long.

Arctic tern

Migratory geese

Canada geese that live in northern North America migrate south in winter. They fly in a V-shaped formation, which means that each bird benefits from lift from the bird in front, so they save energy.

Heavyweight swan

The mute swan can weigh as much as 40 pounds (18 kg) and is one of the heaviest flying birds. This swan lives in Europe and central Asia, but it has been introduced in many other parts of the world. Males and females mate for life and build a nest by water.

SPECIAL BEAKS

The shapes of birds' beaks vary depending on their food and feeding methods.

Upcurved beak The avocet has an unusual beak that curves upward. The bird sweeps its beak to and fro in the water to find worms and other creatures.

Avocet

Carrying food The puffin's favorite food is fish such as sand eels, which it catches in dives beneath the water surface. With its large beak, the puffin can catch lots of fish at a time. The beak also allows it to carry 10 or more fish back to its young in the breeding season.

Digging a burrow The puffin also uses its strong beak to dig a burrow on a clifftop where it lays its egg and rears its young.

Atlantic puffin

Longest journey

The arctic tern makes one of the longest migration journeys of any bird. It breeds in the Arctic during the summer and then flies south to Antarctica for summer there. The tern, therefore, experiences more daylight hours than any other bird.

Birds of prey

Powerful feet and claws and a sharp beak for tearing into the victim's flesh make these birds champion killers. In fact, they are some of the fiercest of all predators. All birds of prey are strong flyers, and many species also have amazingly sharp eyesight.

Large eyes for spotting prey

Wings swept back to streamline the body for maximum speed

Curved talons for attacking and killing

Speedster

The peregrine falcon makes astonishing plunge dives to catch prey in midair. When hurtling through the air toward its victim, the falcon moves at 124 miles (200 km) an hour. That's about twice as fast as a cheetah—the world's champion runner.

Sharp-eyed hunters

Most eagles and buzzards soar over open country, watching for prey with their exceptionally keen eyesight and then swooping down to attack. Other birds of prey, such as goshawks, hunt in the trees, leaping from perch to perch ready to pounce on prey.

DID YOU KNOW? A golden eagle has more than 7,000 feathers!

Eagle-eyed

The mighty bald eagle has wings that measure up to 8 feet (2.4 m) across. It can spot a fish in the water from more than 3,000 feet (1 km) away, then swoops down at high speed to seize its prey in its huge claws.

Broad wings for soaring

The bald eagle builds the biggest nest of any bird. The largest known was 20 feet (6 m) deep—big enough for a giraffe to hide in!

DEADLY WEAPONS

A bird of prey uses its sharp talons to seize and kill prey.

The harpy eagle has the biggest talons of all birds of prey—the size of a grizzly bear's claws. They're an awesome 5 inches (13 cm) long—that's about the length of a biro pen. The harpy's grip is strong enough to break an adult's arm.

5 inches (13 cm)

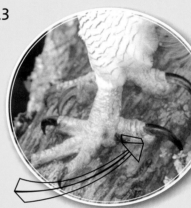

SCAVENGERS

Vultures don't hunt like other birds of prey. They swoop down on dead creatures—sometimes another animal's kill—and grab what they can—even bones!

Andean condor This New World vulture is one of the heaviest of all flying birds and weighs up to 26 or even 33 pounds (12 to 15 kg). It also has one of the largest wing areas of any bird.

. . . .

Old World vultures The many kinds of vultures that live in Africa and Asia have bare heads like the condor. This allows them to plunge their heads into carcasses without getting their feathers soiled.

Snail kite's specially shaped beak

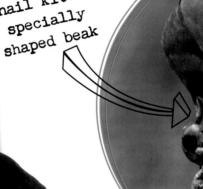

Snails for lunch?

Did you know that there is one bird of prey that feeds mostly on snails? The snail kite's beak is specially shaped for pulling the snail's flesh out of its shell.

Nest building

Some birds just lay their eggs on the ground, but most make a nest. They build the nest as a safe place for their eggs while they incubate and for their young while they grow and develop. Trees are a favorite place for nests, from the neat little cup made by the chaffinch to the untidy mass of sticks built by the stork. Other birds such as hornbills and quetzals nest in tree holes, while the burrowing owl and the Manx shearwater nest in burrows on the ground. The emperor penguin is one bird that does without a nest altogether. The male keeps the egg, then the chick, warm on his own feet.

Tree hole nest

Both male and female quetzals share the work of digging out a nest hole in a tree trunk or branch. The female lays two or three eggs, and the male helps to incubate them. His tail feathers are so long that they stick out of most nest holes.

A chaffinch usually lays four or five eggs, which she incubates for 11 to 13 days. Her mate helps her feed the chicks, which leave the nest at 12 to 15 days.

Cup nest

Like many songbirds, the chaffinch builds a cup-shaped nest in a tree. The nest is made of plant material, such as moss, lichen, and grass, all bound together with spiderwebs.

Woven nest

One of the most beautiful of all nests is made by the weaver bird. The male builds the nest, using strips torn from blades of grass. He starts with a ring-shaped frame and carefully weaves the nest, using as many as 1,000 strips of grass. Females choose males who have made the best nests.

Nest of sticks

Storks build a large nest of branches and twigs lined with grass, rags, and even paper. The nest is often in a tree, but some storks make their nests on chimneys, roofs, or even power pylons. The nest may be used year after year and added to each time, until some are more than 6 feet (2 m) across.

Cliff nests

Cliff swallows nest in groups. They build bowl-shaped nests from mud and plant matter, with a little entrance on one side. The nest is lined with grass and feathers and positioned on a steep cliff or wall where it is very hard for predators to get access to the swallow eggs or the young.

Pigeons, cranes, and relatives

Pigeons and doves are plump birds with dense, soft plumage; small heads; and short legs. There are more than 300 species, most of which feed on seeds and fruit. One unusual feature of pigeons and doves is that unlike other birds, they can drink without tipping their head back.

Cranes are long-necked, long-legged birds that are found all over the world, often around wetlands. Their relatives include bustards, trumpeters, and sun bitterns, as well as smaller birds such as rails, coots, and moorhens, which also live in wetlands.

Moorhen

Mating dance

Both male and female crowned cranes have attractive golden crests. They perform an elaborate courtship dance, during which the birds nod their heads and jump into the air. Like all cranes, this bird eats a wide range of food, including grasses, seeds, and insects.

Crested pigeon

The biggest and one of the most beautiful of all pigeons is the Victoria crowned pigeon, which lives in New Guinea rain forests. It is about the size of a turkey and has blue-gray and red plumage and a lacy crest on its head.

PIGEON "MILK"

Did you know that pigeons and doves feed their young with a kind of milk from their own bodies?

Most birds have to gather food for their young—or show them where to find it. Both male and female pigeons and doves make a milky substance in a pouch called the crop, inside the body, and feed it to their young.

A wood pigeon feeding her young crop "milk."

UNIQUE BIRDS

The sun-grebe and the limpkin are related to cranes and have some very unusual features.

Sun-grebe

Safety pouch There are only three species in the sun-grebe family. The male sun-grebe has a unique way of carrying his young. Under each wing he has a little pouch of skin in which he can carry his chicks in safety, even while in flight.

Snail eater The limpkin lives in marshy areas, and its long beak is adapted for feeding on snails. The beak is rather like a pair of tweezers, with a little gap just before the tip, and it is slightly twisted at the end. The bird can slip its beak into the snail's shell, cut through the muscle, and remove the flesh with ease.

Limpkin

Biggest flyer

The great bustard is generally thought to be the heaviest of all flying birds. Males can weigh as much as 35 pounds (16 kg), and the heaviest known bustard was over 44 pounds (20 kg). In the breeding season, males show off their magnificent tail plumes and whiskers.

Water carrier

Sandgrouse are related to pigeons. They live in dry parts of Africa and Asia and have a special way of making sure their young have enough to drink. The parent bird soaks its belly feathers in water and flies back to the nest. The young suck the water from the feathers.

The feathers on the sandgrouse's belly are adapted to soak up water and can hold as much as 0.7 ounces (20 milliliters).

The passenger pigeon was once the most common bird on Earth, but it was hunted to extinction in North America in the 19th century. ⚠️

Owls, cuckoos, and nightjars

Silent and deadly, owls are expert nighttime predators. They have keen eyesight that helps them see in poor light and exceptional hearing for tracking prey. Members of the nightjar family, such as potoos and poorwills, are also active at night or at dusk, when they catch insects in the air with the help of their large mouths. Cuckoos and their relatives are a varied group, but all have feet with two toes pointing forward and two backward that help them climb well.

Expert ears

The great gray owl lives in the forests of the far north. Even when snow is thick on the ground, the owl can hear the tiniest movement of an animal such as a vole on the ground. The owl then swoops down to catch it in its powerful talons.

NIGHT HUNTERS

Special features make owls the most efficient nocturnal hunters in the bird world.

Owl feather

Fluffy feathers Most birds have hard-edged feathers that make a noise as they fly. Owl feathers have fluffy, fringelike edges that make no noise, allowing the bird to fly silently and ambush prey.

Super sight Owls have large eyes that are far more sensitive in low light levels than human eyes are. An owl can also turn its head 270 degrees, enabling it to see almost all around itself.

Precision hearing In complete darkness, owls depend on their ears and can pinpoint prey with amazing accuracy.

Snowy owl

In hiding

Like most of its family, the potoo is active at night and rests during the day in trees, where its amazing camouflage keeps it safe. The bird's plumage matches the color of the tree trunk, and the bird holds its head and body in such as way that it appears to be simply a tree stump and is very hard to spot.

A VERY SMELLY BIRD!

The hoatzin lives in the Amazon jungle and feeds on leaves, flowers, and fruit.

Its food ferments in the hoatzin's stomach, and this process causes the bird to smell like manure! There is only one species, which may or may not be related to cuckoos.

Hoatzin chicks are also unusual in that they have claws on each wing that help them grip.

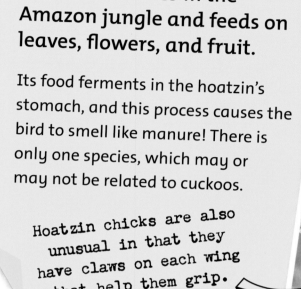

The great gray owl is one of the largest owls and has a wingspan of up to 5 feet (1.5 m).

26 mph/42 kph

Nest invader

Many, but not all, cuckoos lay their eggs in the nest of another bird and leave the host to hatch and rear their young. This reed warbler is feeding a much larger cuckoo chick, which has pushed the warbler young out of the nest.

Fast runner

The greater roadrunner, a member of the cuckoo family, runs faster than any other flying bird. It lives in the American desert, where it speeds along at up to 26 miles (42 km) an hour as it hunts insects, lizards, and snakes.

DID YOU KNOW? The common poorwill hibernates for five months of the year!

Hummingbirds, swifts, and kingfishers

Hummingbirds and swifts might look very different from each other, but both are small, fast-flying birds with tiny legs. Swifts are found in most parts of the world, but hummingbirds live only in North and South America, usually in tropical areas. Kingfishers are generally colorful birds with large heads and strong beaks. They are the best known of their group, but their relatives include birds as varied as hornbills, motmots, and bee-eaters. Most are predators, taking prey such as fish, insects, and other birds, but hornbills also eat fruit.

Ruby-throated hummingbird

Acrobats in the air

Hummingbirds are some of the smallest of all birds and among the most acrobatic in the air. They can fly backward as well as forward and hover as they feed on nectar from flowers. The sword-billed hummingbird has a beak that is up to 4 inches (11 cm) long for feeding from deep flowers. The bird also eats insects.

LIFE ON THE WING

The swift is probably the most aerial of all birds and eats, sleeps, and even mates in the air.

Once a young swift leaves its nest, it may not come to land again for several years, until it is time to rear its own young. A swift's legs are tiny, and it cannot perch but can only cling to surfaces with its claws.

Bee-eater

As its name suggests, the bee-eater feeds mostly on stinging insects such as bees and wasps. It often catches its prey in the air, returns to its perch, and then wipes the insect against the branch to remove its sting.

Sword-billed hummingbird

Bee hummingbird

Hummingbirds move their wings faster than any other bird. Many have been recorded making more than 80 wingbeats a second.

Plunge diver

Despite its beautiful iridescent plumage, the shy kingfisher is rarely seen. It usually lives near rivers and streams and perches above the water to watch for prey. When it spots a fish, the kingfisher plunge dives into the water to seize its catch.

Wings held back to streamline the body

Long, daggerlike beak for seizing fish

RELATIVES

The kingfisher group includes a range of interesting and very different-looking birds.

Hornbills Great Indian hornbills live in Africa and Asia. They nest in a tree hole, and the male seals the female and her eggs into the nest with mud. He then passes food to her through a narrow opening.

Great Indian hornbill

Hoopoe This bird has a very dirty, smelly nest—thought to be a way of keeping predators away from its young.

Motmots Colorful motmots live in forests and gardens in Central and South America. Most have long tails with central feathers that have racquet-shaped tips.

DID YOU KNOW? The laughing kookaburra is the biggest member of the kingfisher family!

Parrots, woodpeckers, and toucans

Brightly colored parrots dart around the trees in tropical and subtropical areas worldwide. There are about 350 kinds, including cockatoos, lovebirds, macaws, and budgerigars as well as parrots themselves. Most feed on plant material, such as seeds, nuts, and fruit, with their strong hooked beaks. The woodpecker group includes birds such as toucans, jacamars, and barbets. All are tree dwellers and have feet with two toes pointing forward and two backward for easy climbing and perching.

Beautiful deep blue plumage

Largest parrot

The hyacinth macaw is the largest of all the parrots at up to 3 feet (1 m) long. It lives in Central and South America and feeds mainly on nuts and seeds, including palm nuts. Sadly, it is now endangered because so many birds have been captured for the pet trade.

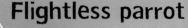

Flightless parrot

The kakapo is the most unusual member of the parrot family. It is the heaviest of all parrots, the only flightless parrot and the only one that is active at night. It also has a strange musty smell. Once common, this bird is now very rare.

The odd couple

In most parrot species, males and females look alike, but not the eclectus parrots. The male is mostly bright green while the female is red and blue. They live in forests in Australia and New Guinea. The pair nests in a tree hole and lays two to four eggs, which the female incubates.

Male eclectus parrot

Female eclectus parrot

Its strong beak can crack even the hardest nuts.

INSECT EATERS

Woodpeckers and some of their relatives have different ways of catching insects.

Aerial hunters Jacamars and puffbirds catch insects such as butterflies and dragonflies in the air, seizing their prey in their long, thin beaks.

Rufous-tailed Jacamar

Drilling for food A woodpecker drills small holes in tree trunks with its powerful beak. The bird then extracts any insects living under the bark with its long sticky tongue.

Foraging on foliage Barbets have strong, stout beaks that they use to search leaves for insects. They also eat some fruit.

Pileated woodpecker

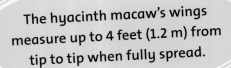

The hyacinth macaw's wings measure up to 4 feet (1.2 m) from tip to tip when fully spread.

KEEPING COOL

Scientists used to think that the toucan's beak was for attracting mates.

Now scientists believe that it is a method of heat control. The beak contains lots of blood vessels, and the bird can control blood flow through the beak to lose or conserve heat as necessary.

The toco toucan's beak is up to 7.4 inches (19 cm) long.

Noisy cockatoos

Sulphur-crested cockatoos are noisy, sociable birds that live in groups or sometimes in flocks of several hundred. They eat the seeds of grasses and other plants as well as insect larvae. Nests are made in tree hollows and the birds lay two to three eggs.

DID YOU KNOW? Woodpeckers have been recorded making 12,000 taps per day as they search for food.

Perching birds

More than half of all types of birds in the world, at least 5,000 species, belong to this group, which is also known as the passerines. It includes birds as varied as wrens, swallows, birds-of-paradise, and crows, but all have feet with three toes pointing forward and one pointing backward. This foot shape is ideal for perching on twigs and posts and the reason for one of the group's common names. The perching birds are believed to be the most intelligent birds, and many show excellent learning abilities. Most feed on insects and seeds, but some, such as shrikes and crows, are also skilled predators.

Great gray shrike

Blue birds

The eastern bluebird, which belongs to the thrush family, and the blue flycatcher both eat insects but have different ways of catching their prey. The bluebird swoops down from its perch to catch insects on the ground. The flycatcher watches for prey, then flies out to catch it in midair.

Yellow breast

The blue tit is a lively little bird that feeds mostly on insects. Females look for mates with very yellow breasts—the yellower the breast, the more caterpillars the bird will have eaten, showing that he will be a good provider for chicks.

POISONOUS BIRD

The only birds known to be poisonous are several species of pitohui, which live in New Guinea.

This was discovered by accident by a researcher who was scratched by one of the birds when releasing it from a trap. The skin and feathers contain a poison that is almost the same as that in poison-dart frogs.

The pitohui takes in the poison from the beetles it eats.

Blue flycatcher

GRACEFUL FLYER

The barn swallow is the most widespread and numerous member of its family.

Barn swallow

Barn swallow Barn swallows are speedy, agile flyers. They catch much of their insect food in the air and swoop down to ponds or rivers to take a drink or splash their feathers.

Nesting These birds make a cup-shaped nest of mud and grass in the corner of a building such as a barn. They feed their young up to 400 times a day.

Migration Barn swallows breed in Europe, Asia, and North America in the summer. They fly south for the winter, making journeys of up to 6,800 miles (11,000 km).

Nesting

Cock of the rock

Jungle bright

The brilliantly colored cock of the rock lives in South America. In the breeding season, males perform group displays to attract the much plainer females. The males hop around and erect their impressive head crests.

Ground nester

The horn lark (also known as the shore lark) looks for a sheltered spot on the ground to make its nest. The nest is made of grass and stems, then lined with soft material such as plant down and hair. The female lark lays two to seven eggs, which she incubates.

Antbird

The shore, or horned, lark is the only lark in North America, where it lives on prairies and around airports as well as shores.

Perching birds

BEAK SHAPES

The shape of a perching bird's beak is a good indication of what it feeds on.

Sunbird

Long, sharp beak Nectar is one of the sunbird's favorite foods. It can plunge its beak into flowers to take nectar or pierce the base from the outside with the tip of its beak to reach the nectar. It also snaps up small insects.

Crossed tips The crossbill has a strange beak with crossed tips. This beak is just the right shape for removing seeds from pine cones—the crossbill's main food. The white-winged crossbill has a slender beak as it feeds from small cones, but the parrot crossbill has a heavy beak for taking seeds from large cones.

Crossbill

Blue bird-of-paradise

Red bird-of-paradise

Raggiana bird-of-paradise

Fabulous feathers

Birds-of-paradise live in the forests of New Guinea and are among the most beautiful of all birds. Males have amazingly varied plumage with special plumes and streamers that they use in elaborate courtship displays to attract females. The female birds are much plainer.

One of the larger perching birds, the hooded crow is 18 inches (47 cm) long and weighs about 1 pound (0.5 kg).

Aerial acrobatics

Starlings are best known for forming huge flocks as they fly back to roosting sites in the early evening, twisting and turning with amazing precision. Each bird sticks close to its neighbor and flies in the same direction, but scientists have found that starlings observe the movements of seven birds around them to anticipate changes of direction.

ATTRACTING A MATE

The male bowerbird doesn't show off his feathers to attract a mate; he builds a pretty bower.

The male of each species of bowerbird builds a bower of a different shape and decorates it as beautifully as he can. The bower is only used for courtship. The birds make a proper nest for their eggs and young.

Satin bowerbirds like to use blue decorations for their bowers.

Clever crows

Crows are intelligent birds. They eat whatever they can find, including prey, plant matter, and carrion. Some crows have been seen dropping shellfish on rocks to smash them open, and in scientific experiments, crows have worked out ways of using tools to get what they want.

DID YOU KNOW? A group of crows is called a murder of crows.

REPTILES & AMPHIBIANS

Tortoises and turtles

Nearly all these reptiles have a hard shell made out of bone and covered with plates of horn to protect the soft body. They don't have teeth but use their sharp-edged jaws to snap up prey or feed on plants. Tortoises live on land while turtles are found in the sea and in freshwater. Terrapins are small turtles that live in and around water. There are more than 250 different kinds of tortoises and turtles.

Marine turtles

Of the seven species of marine turtles, three are in serious danger of becoming extinct and all are rare. These huge sea-living reptiles swim with the help of their long flippers. They spend all of their lives in water, but they do have to come to the surface to breathe. Females haul themselves onto land to lay their eggs in pits on the seashore.

LONG LIFE

Galápagos giant tortoises are the longest lived of all vertebrate animals.

Most live to be more than 100, and the record age is 175. These huge creatures are up to 4 feet (1.2 m) long and weigh over 440 pounds (200 kg). They lead peaceful lives, feeding on leaves and other plant material.

Some of these giant tortoises have a curved shell, allowing them to stretch up to reach leaves.

Snake neck

The snake-necked turtle lives in freshwater and has a neck almost as long as its body. It lies in wait for prey with its long neck folded back, then lunges at any victim that comes near. If attacked, the turtle releases a smelly fluid from special glands.

Loggerhead turtle

Hawksbill turtle

NESTING TURTLES

Every two or three years, female green turtles come to land to lay their eggs.

Female laying eggs

Long migration Turtles may migrate hundreds of miles to lay eggs on the beaches where they hatched.

Laying eggs The female turtle digs a pit in the sand with her flippers. She lays 100 or more eggs, then covers them up and returns to the sea.

Dangerous journey About 65 days later, the baby turtles break out of their shells and make their way to the sea. Many are captured by predators, such as seabirds, on the way.

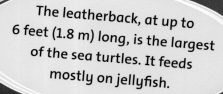

Baby turtle on its way to the sea

The leatherback, at up to 6 feet (1.8 m) long, is the largest of the sea turtles. It feeds mostly on jellyfish.

Power jaws

The fearsome alligator snapping turtle is the largest freshwater turtle. It lies on the riverbed with its mouth open to reveal a pink flap of skin. Fish are attracted to this "lure," thinking it might be good to eat. When a fish comes to have a closer look, the alligator turtle snaps it up in its powerful jaws.

Clever camouflage

The matamata lives in rivers such as the Amazon in South America and has a knobbly shell and a strange-shaped head with flaps of skin. It looks like a pile of dead leaves and debris as it lies on the riverbed, watching for prey.

The hawksbill turtle is rare because of its shell, used to make tortoiseshell jewelry.

Crocodiles and alligators

Some of the fiercest of all predators belong to this group of reptiles. These powerful sharp-toothed hunters live in water and on land, and they prey on anything from fish to buffalo. All are expert swimmers and can also move surprisingly fast on land. There are about 14 species of crocodile, eight of alligators and caimans, and just one gharial. They all live in tropical and subtropical areas of the world, usually in freshwater.

The saltwater crocodile is up to 15 feet (5 m) long and the biggest of the crocodilians. It weighs as much as 990 pounds (450 kg).

Deadly predators

Nile crocodiles and saltwater crocodiles, known as "salties," are the biggest and most ferocious of all reptiles. They lie in the water, with only eyes and nostrils visible above the surface, ready to attack any prey that comes near—including animals larger than themselves. The crocodile surges up and grabs its victim, then holds it underwater until it drowns.

THE CAIMANS

The six species of caiman live in and around lakes and rivers in Central and South America.

Biggest The black caiman is the biggest of the crocodilians in South America. It can grow to more than 13 feet (4 m) long and weighs more than several people.

Broad snout Caimans and their close relatives alligators have broader, shorter snouts than crocodiles.

Stripy babies The stripy pattern on a baby caiman helps it hide from predators among grasses and other plants while it is very small. The stripes gradually fade as the caiman grows.

Young caiman

A crocodile's ears and eyes are on top of its head so it can see and breathe while keeping most of its body underwater.

CARING PARENT

Crocodiles are surprisingly devoted parents.

The female crocodile lays her eggs in a pit she digs near water and stays nearby to guard the eggs while they incubate. When the young are ready to hatch, they call out to their mother, who uncovers the nest and helps the young break out of their shells if necessary. She then carries them to water.

Nile crocodile cracking egg

A Nile crocodile has about 60 teeth, and new ones grow to replace any that are lost or become damaged.

Long jaws

The gharial lives in Indian rivers but is now very rare, and there may be only a few hundred left in the wild. The long, thin jaws, studded with sharp teeth, are ideal for seizing fish, the gharial's main prey.

Swamp hunters

The American alligator lives in the southern United States in swamps, rivers, and marshes. It can grow to 15 feet (4.5 m) long and is an expert hunter, preying on fish, turtles, birds—anything it can get. Once rare because of hunting, the alligator is now thriving.

DID YOU KNOW? Crocodiles can't chew but are thought to swallow stones to help break up their food.

Boas and pythons

The largest and some of the deadliest of all snakes—the mighty pythons and the anaconda—belong to this group. They are not venomous but all are constrictors, which means that they kill by squeezing their victims with their strong body coils until their victims suffocate. Pythons lay eggs, like most snakes, but a female boa keeps her developing eggs inside her and gives birth to fully formed live young.

Boa

Tree dweller

The brilliantly colored emerald tree boa lives in trees in the Amazon rain forest. It coils itself around a branch and holds on tight with its prehensile (gripping) tail while it lunges out to catch passing prey. It seizes victims in its sharp teeth but kills by constriction.

PYTHONS

These constrictors live in Africa, Asia, and Australia and its surrounding islands.

"Seeing" heat Pythons often hunt at night, and many have heat-sensitive pits along their upper lip. These help the snake track down warm-bodied prey by detecting the heat they give off.

Carpet python

Good mothers Pythons are among the few snakes that look after their eggs. The female Indian python curls herself around her clutch of eggs and keeps them warm with her own body. She can raise the temperature by contracting her muscles to make shivering movements.

Python guarding her eggs

Heavyweight snake

The anaconda is the world's heaviest snake and can weigh up to 550 pounds (250 kg)—as much as three or four people. It spends much of its life in water and hunts at night for large prey such as deer, capybaras, and even caiman.

Colubrids

As many as two-thirds of all snakes belong to this family, which contains more than 1,600 species, including garter snakes, grass snakes, and king snakes. All have a large mouth and can open their jaws wide to swallow big prey. Some colubrids are venomous, but their fangs are located toward the back of the mouth. This makes them less dangerous to humans than front-fanged snakes.

The boomslang lives in trees and preys on birds and lizards.

Shedding skin

Snakes shed their skin at least once a year to reveal new skin underneath. The skin starts coming away at the top of the head, then the snake rubs against something until the whole skin peels off like a sock.

EGG EATER

Did you know that there is a snake that specializes in eating birds' eggs?

The egg-eating snake can open its jaws very wide and take a whole egg into its mouth. When the egg reaches the snake's throat, it is pierced by special bony projections and the contents are swallowed. The snake then regurgitates the eggshell.

Dangerous snake

The African boomslang is one of the most venomous of the colubrids. Its venom prevents the victim's blood from clotting so is highly dangerous. If alarmed, the boomslang puffs up its neck to make itself look bigger.

The egg-eating snake has no teeth.

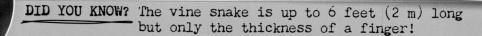

DID YOU KNOW? The vine snake is up to 6 feet (2 m) long but only the thickness of a finger!

Cobras

All cobras and their relatives—mambas, taipans, and sea snakes—are venomous and highly dangerous. Their fangs are positioned at the front of the mouth, which makes it easy for them to strike prey and inject their venom at a high speed. The fangs are fixed to the upper jawbone, so they cannot be very long or the snake would not be able to close its mouth without piercing its lower jaw.

Superfast

One of the world's deadliest snakes, the black mamba may also be the fastest and can move at up to 12 miles (20 km) an hour. Only the inside of its mouth is black, and it shows this when alarmed.

Spitting venom

Spitting cobras have a very special way of discouraging attackers. They can spit out venom that can cause blindness if it reaches the victim's eyes.

COPYCAT SNAKE

The next best thing to being venomous is to look like a dangerous creature.

The bright stripes of the eastern coral snake signal that it has a venomous bite. The milk snake, which belongs to the colubrid group of snakes, is harmless, but its colorful markings mean that predators steer clear—just in case!

Eastern coral snake

Milk snake

King of snakes

At about 18 feet (5.5 m) in length, the king cobra is the longest venomous snake. It can raise about a third of its length up off the ground to face an attacker and spread out the skin beneath its head. Enough venom is delivered in one bite to kill an elephant.

DID YOU KNOW? The king cobra feeds almost entirely on other snakes!

Vipers

The snakes with the most sophisticated venom equipment are the vipers. Their fangs are positioned near the front of the mouth but lie folded back when not in use. When the snake wants to strike, the fangs swing forward as the mouth opens. This means that vipers can have longer fangs than other snakes. Most vipers hunt by ambushing their prey and have markings that help to camouflage them as they lie in wait for their victims.

NIGHT HUNTERS

Special features make vipers perfectly equipped nighttime predators.

Sensory pits Pit vipers, such as the bushmaster and rattlesnakes, have a heat-sensitive pit on each side of the head, between the eyes and the nose. These allow the snakes to find warm-blooded prey in complete darkness and strike accurately.

Bushmaster's head

Long fangs Gaboon vipers have longer fangs than any other snake. They can measure as much as 2 inches (5 cm)—nearly as long as an adult person's little finger.

Gaboon **viper** fangs

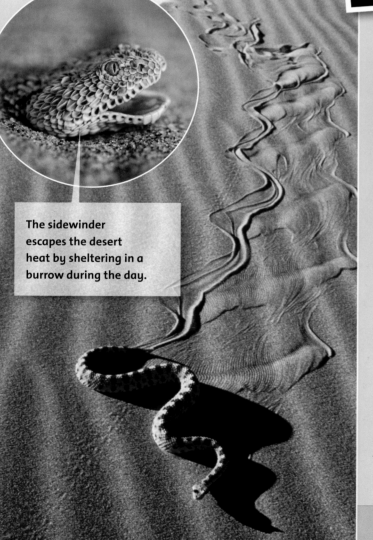

The sidewinder escapes the desert heat by sheltering in a burrow during the day.

Desert travel

The sidewinder snake lives in the desert and has developed a special way of traveling over sand. It moves itself along sideways by pushing against the only two sections of its body that touch the ground.

Warning sound

Rattlesnakes, such as the eastern diamondback, warn off enemies by shaking the "rattle" at the end of their tail to make a buzzing noise. The rattle is made of hard rings of skin, and one ring is added each time the snake sheds its skin.

Venom and poison

Both venom and poison can be deadly, but there is a difference between them. A *poisonous* animal contains a toxic substance in a part of its body, such as its skin, which harms anything that eats or touches it. The poison is generally used for defense, rather than attacking prey. A *venomous* animal must inject its deadly chemicals, usually made in glands, into the victim by means of a fang, a spine, or other device. The venom is mainly used for killing prey but may also be used against an attacker. Sea snakes are some of the most venomous of all animals, but fortunately humans rarely come across them.

Venomous bite

The gila monster lives in the deserts of the American Southwest and is one of the world's very few venomous lizards. This 20-inch-long (50 cm) reptile kills by biting its prey and then chewing while venom flows from its mouth into the wound.

A rattlesnake's hollow fangs are linked to its venom glands.

Toxic spray

The painted salamander has an unusual way of defending itself. If attacked, it flicks its tail toward the enemy, spraying it with a toxic liquid made by glands near the base of the tail. The salamander generally aims at the attacker's face and eyes, and the liquid causes pain but not death.

The bright colors of poison-dart frogs warn potential predators that they risk a nasty mouthful and even death if they attack.

Danger alert

Poison-dart frogs are tiny but deadly. The poison is contained in the skin and probably comes from the insects that the frogs eat. The most dangerous of these little frogs contain enough poison to kill ten or more people.

Iguanas and relatives

Green iguana

Rhinoceros iguana

Some of the most interesting and colorful lizards belong to this group, which is divided into three families—iguanas, agamids, and chameleons. The iguanas are the largest of the three families and has more than 1,000 species. All these lizards have four legs, and nearly all hunt other creatures, usually insects, to eat. They hunt during the day by sight and capture their prey with their large tongue. Many have crests or flaps of skin on the head that they use when showing off to potential mates or threatening rivals. Most run and climb well, but chameleons are particularly well adapted to life in the trees.

Land iguanas

Iguanas range in size from about 4 inches (10 cm) to huge creatures of up to 6 feet (2 m). Most live in North, Central, and South America, but there are some species in Fiji and Madagascar. Many perform elaborate displays with movements of their head, tail, or skin flaps to attract mates or challenge enemies.

AGAMID LIZARDS

More than 350 kinds of agamid lizard live in Africa, Australia, and warmer parts of Asia.

Spiky protection The thorny devil moves slowly, but its body is covered with so many spines and spikes that it is very hard for any predator to attack. This lizard feeds almost entirely on ants.

Thorny devil

Frill display The amazing frilled lizard lives in Australia. If in danger, it spreads the skin flaps around its neck to make itself look much larger than it really is.

Frilled lizard

Parson's chameleon is up to 2 feet (60 cm) long and one of the largest chameleons. Its tongue is twice the length of its body.

Sea lizard

Marine iguanas, which live on the Galápagos Islands off the coast of South America, are the only sea lizards. They feed on seaweed, which they scrape off rocks on the shore or gather underwater.

Male marine iguanas dive down as far as 30 feet (10 m) when looking for seaweed.

WALKING ON WATER

The green basilisk lizard can run a short distance across water!

If threatened by a predator, the lizard escapes across water, running so fast that it stays on the surface. Little bubbles form beneath its long-toed feet, and the lizard pushes off against these before they burst.

Green basilisk lizard

The feet have three clawed toes on one side and two on the other to help grip.

Eyes can swivel and point in different directions so the chameleon can see as much as possible.

Chameleons

The color-changing ability of chameleons has more to do with mood than camouflage. If a chameleon is angry or threatened, it may change color to trick its enemy. Males looking for a mate become much brighter in color. Chameleons catch their prey by shooting out their long sticky-tipped tongue to trap prey.

DID YOU KNOW? The pygmy chameleon is only up to 3 inches (7 cm) long, including its tail!

The orange-tailed skink of Mauritius is critically endangered, mostly because of introduced predators.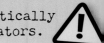

Geckos, skinks, and relatives

Leopard gecko

Tokay gecko

From tiny, agile geckos to huge monitor lizards such as the Komodo dragon, lizards are extraordinarily successful creatures that have managed to adapt to life in habitats as varied as deserts and rain forests. Like other reptiles, most reproduce by laying eggs, but a few, such as the viviparous lizard of Europe and Asia, retain their eggs inside the body and give birth to live young. Nearly all lizards communicate by movements or signals, but geckos make a range of sounds to attract mates or warn off rivals.

Geckos

These little nocturnal lizards live all over the world in tropical and subtropical regions. Most have a slightly flattened body and enormous eyes to help them see in poor light. Thousands of tiny hairs on the underside of their toes help them climb on smooth surfaces, and they can even walk along upside down.

Komodo dragon

The Komodo dragon can weigh up to 290 pounds (130 kg)—more than two people—and is the heaviest of all lizards. It ambushes prey as large as buffalo and will also eat carrion—and even other Komodo dragons!

A Komodo dragon has an excellent sense of smell, which helps it track down prey. It kills with its venomous bite.

Web-footed gecko

Special webbed toes help this gecko to run across the surface of desert sand without sinking.

Sandfish

Eyed skink

SPOT THE GECKO!

The leaf-tailed gecko looks so much like a dead leaf that it is almost impossible to spot.

If an attacker does see the gecko and grabs it by the tail, it can shed its tail and grow a new one. This gecko usually preys on insects at night.

The gecko even has markings like leaf veins and irregular edges that look like they have been nibbled.

LEGLESS LIZARDS

There are many kinds of lizard that have no legs and look more like snakes and worms.

Slow worm This lizard lives in parts of Europe, Asia, and North Africa. It is generally active at night and can lose its tail if attacked. The tail is usually regrown but slowly.

Glass lizard At more than 3 feet (1 m) long, at least half of which is tail, this lizard is longer than many snakes. Slugs and snails are its main food.

California legless lizard This nocturnal reptile lives just under loose soil and is rarely seen on the surface. It preys on insects.

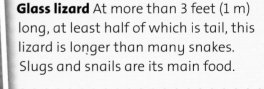

Glass lizard

Skinks

The skinks are one of the largest families of lizards, with about 1,500 species. A typical skink has a long body and tail and short legs, but some have very tiny legs or none at all. Skinks generally live on the ground or in burrows and feed on insects and other small creatures. A few species feed on plants.

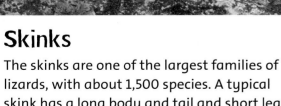

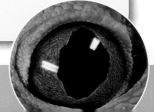

The largest amphibian, the Chinese giant salamander, is now rare due to hunting and habitat destruction. ⚠

Newts and salamanders

Most amphibians spend at least part of their life in water. Newts and salamanders are amphibians, like frogs and toads. Nearly all have a long body and tail and four legs, although some salamanders have only very tiny legs. Some salamanders live in water, others on land, while most newts live on land but breed in water. Like frogs, newts and salamanders lay eggs that hatch into swimming tadpoles with gills for breathing in water.

This newt has four toes on its front feet and five on its back feet.

Each great crested newt has slightly different markings.

CAECILIANS

These wormlike creatures are actually amphibians. There are more than 100 species, some of which are over 6 feet (2 m) long. Most live in burrows, but a few are aquatic.

Life underground A caecilian has no limbs and digs its burrow with the help of its pointy head. It has lots of sharp teeth that it uses to catch worms and insects as well as other amphibians. It has tiny eyes—or none at all—but finds its food with the help of sensory tentacles on its head.

Food The female feeds her young with secretions from her body, but her young also eat her fat-rich skin. She regrows her skin to keep up their food supplies.

Bearded caecilian

Breeding signals

The male great crested newt develops a spiky crest along his back in the breeding season to attract a mate and also signals to females by fanning his tail and performing a display dance. When he finds a mate, he deposits a package of sperm, which she picks up. The female lays her eggs on leaves for protection, and the eggs hatch into tadpoles.

Caecilian

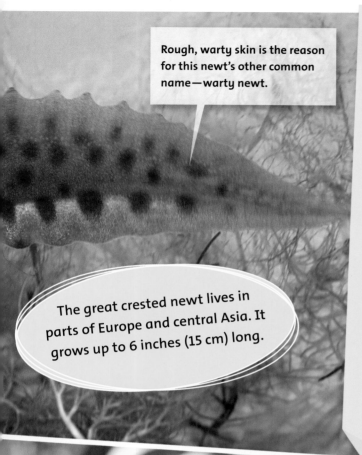

Rough, warty skin is the reason for this newt's other common name—warty newt.

The great crested newt lives in parts of Europe and central Asia. It grows up to 6 inches (15 cm) long.

FOREVER YOUNG

The axolotl is a type of salamander that remains a larva throughout its life.

Most amphibians lose the feathery gills they have as tadpoles, but the axolotl keeps them and does not develop into adult form. It can still mate and bear young, however. Axolotls live only in one lake in Mexico and are now rare. They grow to about 1 foot (30 cm) and feed mostly on worms, insect larvae, and shellfish.

Large feathery gills allow the axolotl to breathe in water.

Fierce predator

The tiger salamander is the largest of all land-living salamanders and can grow up to 14 inches (35 cm) long. It shelters in burrows made by crayfish or other creatures. At night it comes out to hunt worms, insects, and even small mammals such as mice.

Stream dweller

The hellbender spends its whole life in water, usually clear, fast-flowing streams. This giant salamander grows up to 30 inches (74 cm) long. In the breeding season, the male makes a shallow nest under a rock or a log where the female lays her eggs. The male guards the eggs while they develop.

Olm

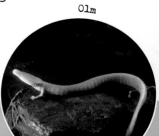

DID YOU KNOW? The olm lives in caves in total darkness for up to 50 years.

Frogs and toads

Like most amphibians, frogs and toads live in water and on land. They swim and hop, and some can even climb with ease. A typical frog has a large head, a short body, and long back legs, but no tail. All adult frogs and toads catch creatures such as insects to eat, and larger species prey on fish, birds, and even mice. Their young—tadpoles—feed on plants, although some prey on insect larvae and other tadpoles.

Frog spawn

Tadpole

Tadpole with back legs

Egg to adult

Most frogs lay their eggs in water. The eggs, which have a jellylike coating to keep them safe, hatch into little swimming creatures called tadpoles. The tadpoles have a long tail and feathery gills for breathing in water. As the tadpoles grow, they develop legs and lungs, and their gills and tail eventually disappear.

BIGGEST FROG

The goliath frog is the world's largest, and it lives in African rain forests.

Its body is at least 11 inches (30 cm) long, and it weighs more than 6.5 pounds (3 kg). Strangely, its eggs and tadpoles are no bigger than those of other, smaller frogs. The world's tiniest frog lives in New Guinea and is only 0.3 inches (7 millimeters) long.

Goliath frogs eat insects, fish, shellfish, and other frogs.

Toad pests

Cane toads come from Central and South America but were taken to Australia to control pests in sugarcane plantations. Unfortunately, the toads spread so successfully that they are now themselves considered pests and have destroyed many Australian species.

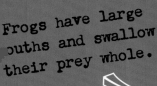

Frogs have large mouths and swallow their prey whole.

Adult bullfrog

GUARDING YOUNG

Most frogs lay their eggs in water. Some, however, have very special ways of caring for eggs and their young, so they don't have to live near water.

Marsupial frog

Breeding pouches The marsupial frog lays her eggs on damp ground. Her mate guards them until they hatch, then takes the tadpoles into little pouches on his body, where they grow and develop into frogs.

Darwin's frog

Mouth brooder The male Darwin's frog takes his tadpoles into a special pouch near his throat, where they remain until they have grown into fully developed froglets.

Feeling for food

The Surinam toad spends nearly all its life in shallow muddy ponds, where its flattened shape helps it stay out of sight. Its eyes are very small, but it feels for food with the help of its sensitive fingertips. It feeds by simply opening its mouth and taking in prey and water.

Climbing frogs

The red-eyed tree frog shelters under a leaf and sleeps during the day, then wakes up at night to find prey. Lots of birds and snakes hunt these frogs, and they may startle predators with a flash of their huge red eyes. Tree frogs are expert climbers with the help of large rounded toe pads.

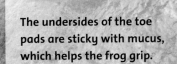
The undersides of the toe pads are sticky with mucus, which helps the frog grip.

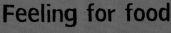

DID YOU KNOW? The glass frog's skin is so thin that you can see its internal organs!

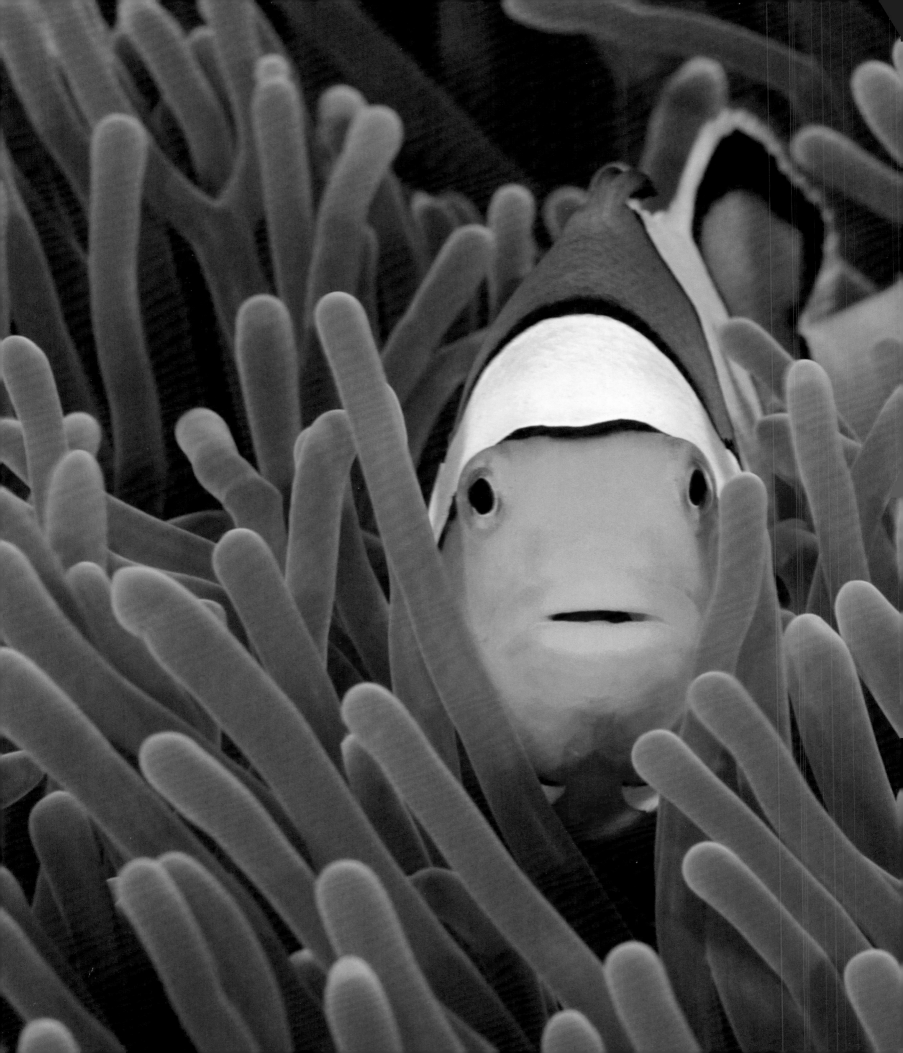

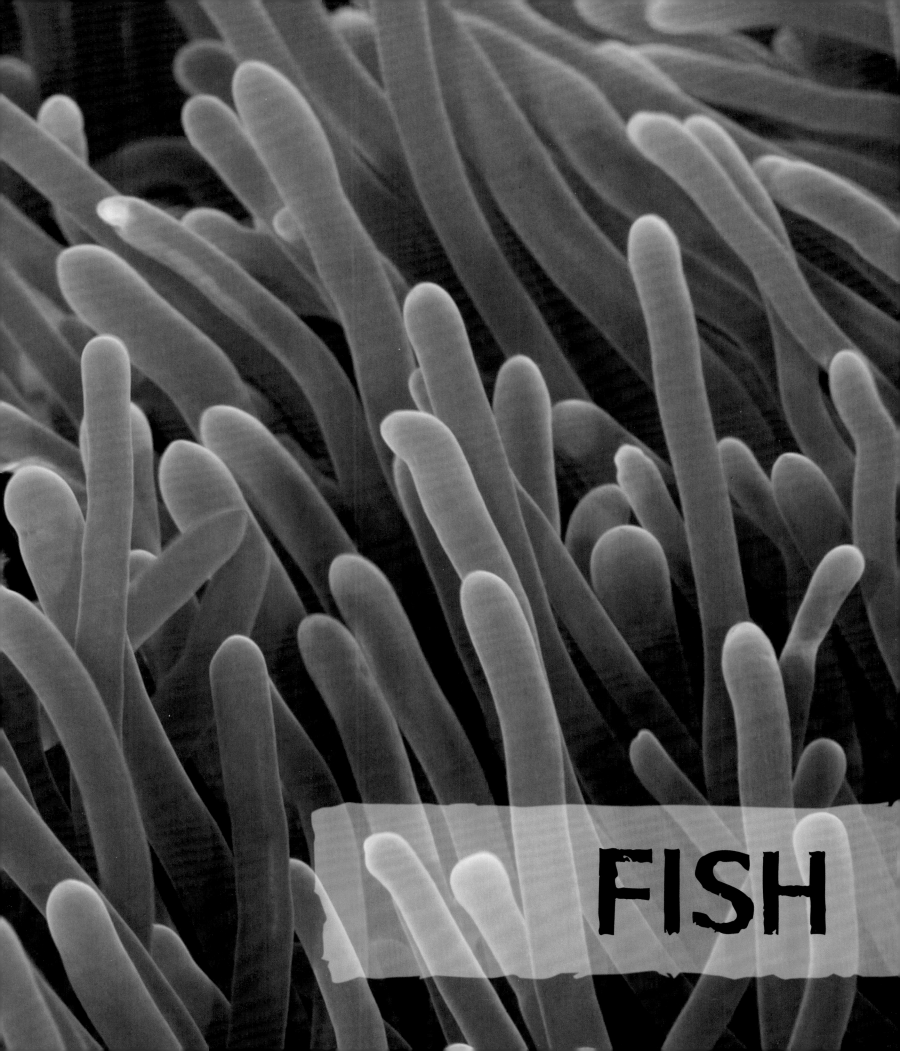

FISH

Sharks and rays

The fiercest of all ocean hunters are the sharks. Most of these fish are large, fast-moving predators with sharp teeth and excellent senses, particularly of smell. But some, such as carpet sharks, are less active and lurk on the seabed, watching for prey to come near. Sharks and their relatives skates and rays are cartilaginous fishes—their skeletons are made of cartilage, a gristly substance. Other fish have bony skeletons.

SWIMMING SCAVENGERS

Tiger sharks have huge appetites and will eat almost anything that comes their way.

Like its namesake, this huge shark is a fierce hunter and can kill more or less anything in its path with its daggerlike teeth. But it is also a scavenger and eats dead animals, as well as gulping down nonfood items such as car tires and metal!

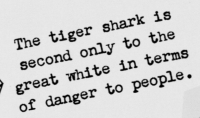

The **tiger shark is** second only to the **great white in terms** of danger to people.

Killer teeth

The great white shark is a supreme hunter. Its streamlined body helps it cut through the water at a high speed, and it kills with the help of its huge teeth, which have serrated edges like bread knives. Its sense of smell is so acute that it can sniff out a drop of blood from more than a mile (1.6 km) away.

Sawfish

RAYS

Rays have a wide, flattened body and fins like wings that they flap to move through the water.

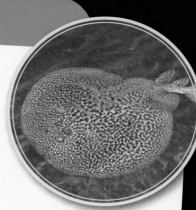

Marbled electric ray

Electric shock The electric ray kills its prey with a powerful shock from its own electric organs.

Toxic weapon The stingray has a sharp spine at the base of its tail that can deliver a dose of powerful venom to any attacker.

Manta rays The manta ray is the world's largest ray and measures an amazing 23 feet (7 m) across. Despite its size, it is not a hunter and feeds by filtering small creatures from the water.

Stingray

Hammerhead shark

The underside of the hammerhead shark's strange-shaped head contains special electrical receptors. These help the shark detect the tiniest electrical fields given off by prey. The stingray, one of its favorite foods, lives buried in the sand, but the hammerhead can search it out with ease.

The large lobes at the sides of the manta's mouth help to funnel food into the mouth but fold back when not in use.

Biggest fish

Not all sharks are ferocious hunters. The whale shark is the biggest of all fish at up to 44 feet (13.5 m) long. It simply swims slowly through the water, taking huge amounts of small fish and other creatures into its wide mouth.

DID YOU KNOW? The sawfish is a type of ray and has up to 32 teeth on each side of its sawlike jaws.

Herrings and eels

Some of the most important of all food fish, such as sardines and anchovies, belong to the herring group, which includes nearly 400 species. Most are small, streamlined fish with silvery scales and forked tails. They live in the sea in groups, or schools, and feed on plankton (tiny creatures floating in the water). There are about 700 species of eels. A typical eel is a long, slender fish, with a fin that runs the length of the back and joins with the tail fin.

Herring

Schooling fish

Anchovies *(above)* and their relatives tend to gather together in huge numbers. A shoal of fish is simply a large group, but a school of fish swims together, changing direction and moving as one with astonishing speed and coordination. There are more than 130 types of anchovies, and most are less than 6 inches (15 cm) long.

Giant moray

Moray eels generally live in warm waters, particularly coral reefs, and have a large mouth and sharp teeth. Many hide during the day and hunt at night. The giant moray eel is the largest at up to 9.8 feet (3 m) long.

MIGRATING EELS

European eels lay their eggs in the Sargasso Sea—more than 3,700 miles (6,000 km) from Europe.

Drifting larvae When the larvae hatch, they gradually drift with the currents to European coasts. The young eels, or elvers, then swim into rivers where they live and grow for as long as 20 years.

Back to the sea Mature eels eventually swim back to the sea and travel back to the Sargasso Sea to breed.

Endangered Once common, European eels are now rare and in danger of extinction.

Young European eels

Carp, catfish, and piranhas

Nearly all of these fish live in freshwater. A common feature of the 3,000 or so species of carp is that these fish do not have teeth in their jaws. Instead, they have special throat teeth, which help them grind down their food. Catfish get their name from the whiskerlike barbels around the mouth. These barbels are covered with taste buds, which help the fish find food. Piranhas live in Central and South America.

Carp

The carp is a large fish that lives in still or slow-moving water. It feeds mostly on plants and small animals, such as worms and insect larvae. It is able to gulp air at the surface so it can survive in water with poor oxygen levels.

Sharp-toothed hunter

The red-bellied piranha is only 1 foot (30 cm) long but is a fierce hunter, with razor-sharp triangular teeth for stripping flesh from its prey. Not all piranhas are deadly predators, however. Some feed only on insects or plants.

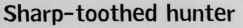

SHOCKING FISH

The electric eel isn't an eel at all but a relative of carp and catfish.

This fish can kill its prey with an electric shock of as much as 600 volts that it makes in special electric organs in its body. Fish, frogs, and sometimes birds are its usual victims. The electric eel can grow up to 8 feet (2.5 m) long.

Mighty catfish

One of the largest freshwater fish, the wels catfish grows up to 10 feet (3 m) long and can weigh 330 pounds (150 kg)—although most are smaller. It preys on worms and other creatures but also eats frogs, rodents, and ducks.

The Mekong giant catfish is now extremely rare and in danger of extinction.

Coral reef fish

Coral reefs form in warm, shallow, clear seas. The corals themselves may look like plants, but in fact, they are animals, and it is their skeletons that make up the reef. Coral reefs are home to more than 4,000 kinds of fish, as well as to many other creatures. The reefs provide plenty of nooks and crannies where fish can hide and shelter, and many reef fish have very flattened bodies that allow them to twist and turn among the coral.

Long snout

The copperband butterflyfish has a long snout for picking small prey from crevices in coral. The black eyespot marking near the tail helps to confuse potential predators.

This little cleaner shrimp is feeding on parasites in the grouper's mouth.

Moorish idols swim near a school of bigeye scad.

Stealthy hunters

Groupers are predatory fish. The grouper lies in wait among coral, watching for prey such as fish or crabs to come close. It then dashes out to seize its victim in its large mouth. This coral grouper grows to about 18 inches (45 cm) long.

Crafty hunter

The smooth trunkfish feeds on small creatures such as worms and shellfish that live hidden on the seabed. The trunkfish blows a jet of water from its mouth into the sand to disturb its prey, then snaps it up before it can escape.

Beaked fish

The blue parrotfish has a sturdy body and grows to about 4 feet (1.2 m) long. Males have a rounded, humped forehead. Like all parrotfish, this species has teeth that are joined into a sharp "beak," which the fish

Sponge eater

The colorful emperor angelfish lives around coral reefs where it feeds mostly on sponges. It has strong jaws and can also crush hard-shelled animals. Young fish look very different from adults and have black and white stripes.

Salmon and relatives

There are sea-living and freshwater fish in this group, while others, such as salmon and trout, spend time in both the sea and rivers. Most salmon-type fish have a long, slender body covered with small scales and are fast swimmers. They prey on other fish and have lots of small sharp teeth. Their relatives the pikes and pickerels are also sharp-toothed predators that live in fresh water. Hatchetfish belong to a separate group of deep-sea fish.

Dangerous journey

Sockeye salmon live in the North Pacific but swim up into the rivers of their birth to breed. The journey can be long, and the fish face dangers such as waterfalls and hungry bears. Normally silvery-colored, breeding males turn bright red.

Salmon leaping up a waterfall

LIVING LIGHTS

Marine hatchetfish live at depths of 650 to 3,000 feet (200 to 1,000 m) where there is little light.

The hatchetfish has its own lights, arranged in rows along each side of the body. These may help to confuse predators and also allow the fish to recognize and signal to its own kind.

This fish has a deep, very flattened body and upturned mouth.

Ambush!

A large freshwater fish with a streamlined body, the pike can grow up to 5 feet (1.5 m) long. Females are larger than males. This powerful predator hunts by lying in wait among water plants, then darting out at a high speed to catch prey that comes near.

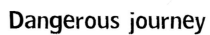

Arctic cha

DID YOU KNOW? The arctic char lives farther north than any other freshwater fish!

Cod and anglers

Nearly all the fish in the cod group, which includes familiar species such as haddock, pollock, and hake, live in the sea, but there are also a few freshwater examples. A typical codfish is long and slender with three fins on its back and two on its underside. Anglerfish look very different from cod, and most have an extremely large mouth and head and a small tapering body. Many have an unusual shape with lots of skin flaps for camouflage.

Flaps resembling seaweed help the sargassum fish stay out of sight.

Breeding time

In the breeding season, a female cod may release up to five million eggs into the water. The eggs hatch in two to four weeks. Young fish feed on plankton (tiny creatures that drift in the water) while adults prey on other fish and shellfish.

LURING PREY

There are more than 200 kinds of anglerfish, many of which live in the deep sea.

Luminous lure Food can be hard to find in the deep sea, but female anglerfish have a special spine above the head that acts as a lure to attract prey. Other fish see the lure, which generally has a luminous tip, and come close to investigate. As soon as the fish is near enough, the anglerfish snaps it up in its huge mouth.

Tiny male The male anglerfish is much smaller than the female. He does not find his own food but lives attached to a female, obtaining food from her body.

Camouflaged fish

The sargassum fish is a type of anglerfish. It lives in warm seas, usually among beds of sargassum seaweed. The fleshy, seaweedlike flaps on its body make the fish very hard to spot. It preys on fish and shrimp that it catches when they come to the sargassum beds to feed.

Blotchy markings and irregular shape help keep the anglerfish hidden as it watches for prey.

Spiny-rayed fish

More than half of all fish belong to this group, which includes more than 14,000 species. The majority live in the sea, everywhere from coral reefs to the dark depths, but there are freshwater species too. Spiny-rayed fish range in size from tiny gobies, which are only about 0.4 inches (1 cm) long, to huge fish such as marlin weighing 1,765 pounds (800 kg). They differ dramatically in appearance, but nearly all have stiff spines in the fins on their backs.

In the breeding season, female perch lay thousands of eggs, which stick together in bands wound around water plants.

Freshwater fish

The perch lives in lakes and rivers in Europe and parts of northern Asia. It has also been introduced into other parts of the world. A sturdy-bodied fish, it grows to about 10 inches (25 cm) long and has two large fins on its back. Young perch eat tiny plankton, but adults hunt larger creatures and other fish.

CLEANER AT WORK

The little cleaner wrasse is only up to 4 inches (11 cm) long but performs a valuable service for other fish.

Cleaner wrasse feed on tiny creatures that live on other fish. They seem to work in pairs, and fish come to the wrasse to have parasites and other debris removed.

A cleaner wrasse is removing parasites from inside the mouth of a larger fish.

Flying fish

SEA HORSES

There are about 35 different kinds of sea horse, living in warm waters worldwide.

Sea horse

Swimming and hiding Sea horses can't swim fast, but they do move themselves along with the help of a small fin on the back. They can also hold onto floating weed with their prehensile tail. Some, such as the sea dragons, have lots of extra skin flaps to help them hide among seaweed.

Breeding habits Sea horses mate for life. The male has a pouch on the front of his body. The female lays her eggs into this pouch, and he carries them while they develop. The eggs hatch into tiny sea horses, which he then releases into the water.

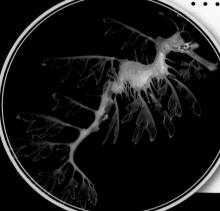

Leafy sea dragon

Making a nest

The three-spined stickleback is one of the few fish that cares for its young. The female lays her eggs in a nest that the male makes from plants. The male then guards the eggs while they develop, fanning them with his fins to provide extra oxygen.

Longest fish

At almost 33 feet (10 m) long, the oarfish is one of the longest of all fish. It's more than twice the length of a family car. This giant lives in seas worldwide but is rarely seen. It feeds on tiny planktonic creatures.

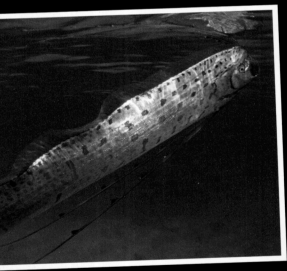

Flying fish?

Flying fish don't really fly, but they can glide over the surface of the sea. After building up speed in the water, the fish leaps above the surface with the help of its large fins and then glides for distances of up to 656 feet (200 m).

Good shot

The little archerfish has an unusual way of catching prey. The fish fires out a jet of water at an insect on an overhanging branch, knocking it into the water. Archerfish do also leap out of the water to catch prey.

DID YOU KNOW? The archerfish can make an accurate hit with its water jet from up to 5 feet (1.5 m) away.

Spiny-rayed fish

The beak is lined with small sharp teeth.

Marlin

High-speed swimmer

One of the fastest of all fish, the streamlined bluefin tuna swims across the ocean at up to 43 miles (70 km) an hour with the help of its powerful tail. Bluefin tuna usually grow to 6 feet (2 m) long and weigh about 550 pounds (250 kg), but giants of 750 pounds (340 kg) or more have been discovered.

Fast and fierce

Marlin and sailfish are speedy swimmers and some of the fiercest of all predatory fish. Both have a very long upper jaw that forms a spearlike beak. When hunting, these fish swim into schools of smaller fish and thrash their sharp beaks from side to side. They wound and stun large numbers of prey, which they then gobble up.

School of predators

The barracuda is a large, long-bodied fish with a pointed head and large mouth full of sharp teeth. It often hunts alone but sometimes gathers in huge schools of hundreds of fish for hunting or possibly for protection from larger predators.

The sailfish may be the speediest of all fish and has been timed swimming at up to 60 miles (100 km) an hour.

HEAVYWEIGHT

Weighing in at up to 4,960 pounds (2,250 kg), the ocean sunfish is the heaviest of all bony fish.

This massive fish is a very strange shape. It is almost round and looks rather like a large head with fins and frilly tail. It swims by moving its fins but cannot move very fast. Jellyfish are its main food, but it also eats small fish.

The ocean sunfish measures up to 10 feet (3.3 m) long.

The sailfish measures up to 11 feet (3.4 m)—as long as two adult humans.

Prickly fish

For much of the time, the porcupine fish has a long, slender body. But if threatened, it can puff itself up dramatically by swallowing lots of water. This causes the sharp spines on its body to erect and make it almost impossible for any predator to swallow.

FLATFISH

The 550 or so species of flatfish have body shapes that suit their lifestyles.

Changing shape A young flatfish hatches with a normal body shape, with an eye on both sides of its head. As it grows, its body flattens sideways and one eye moves so that both are on the upper surface of the body.

Camouflage Flatfish can swim, but they spend much of their time lying on the seabed watching out for enemies and food. With a few wriggles, a flatfish can cover itself with sand.

Halibut on the seabed

INVERTEBRATES

Grasshoppers, dragonflies, and relatives

Shimmering dragonflies are among the most ancient of insect groups, and they have remained virtually unchanged for 300 million years or more. Cockroaches, too, date back to before the days of the dinosaurs. They are extremely adaptable creatures, able to live in almost any conditions. Grasshoppers, crickets, and locusts all have very powerful back legs and can make spectacular leaps to escape from danger.

A grasshopper can leap more than 20 times its own length and can also jump up at least 10 times its length.

A dragonfly can move its four wings independently and beat them about 30 times a second.

A dragonfly breathes through tiny holes along the sides of its long body.

Locusts

FASTEST FLYER

Dragonflies are some of the fastest flying and most acrobatic of all insects.

These beautiful, colorful insects are predators and are skilled at chasing and catching prey in midair. As it flies, a dragonfly holds its front legs out ready to seize other insects such as flies. It can fly backward as well as forward and can reach speeds of up to 24 miles (38 km) an hour.

A dragonfly's large eyes allow it to see almost all around itself.

Cricket

DAMSELFLIES

These insects are relatives of dragonflies but are slower and weaker in the air.

Eyesight Damselflies and dragonflies rely on their excellent eyesight for finding prey.

Damselfly eyes

Eggs and the young Like dragonflies, damselflies lay their eggs in water. The eggs hatch into water-living larvae called nymphs. These nymphs are predators and hunt by shooting out their lower lip to snatch prey such as insects and tadpoles.

Transformation When the nymph is fully grown, it crawls out of the water up onto a plant stem. Its skin splits, and the fully formed adult emerges.

Adult damselfly emerging

Noisy singers

Grasshoppers and crickets are well known for their noisy songs. Some make their sounds by rubbing rough patches on the back wings against the front wings. Others have a scraper on one wing and a ridge on the other. They rub these together to make their song.

Fast hunter

The praying mantis is one of the speediest hunters in the insect world. It lies in wait for prey, then shoots out its spiny front legs to grasp its victim. The meal is back in the mantid's mouth in only a fraction of a second.

Caring mother

The earwig is one of the few insects that takes care of its young. The female guards her eggs while they develop. Once her young hatch, she feeds and protects them until they are old enough to look after themselves.

Cockroaches

A flattened body allows these insects to hide in small crevices. They have wings but rarely fly, preferring to scuttle about on their strong legs. The female lays her eggs into a special container at the end of her body.

Beetles and bugs

With more than 350,000 species, beetles are the biggest insect group and some of the most successful of all animals. They live in virtually every type of habitat and eat everything from other insects to wood, plants, and fur. The word *bug* is often used for insects generally, but bugs are also a particular group of insects that includes aphids, cicadas, and bedbugs. Bugs have special mouthparts for sucking up liquid food.

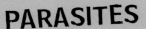

Tiger beetle

When underwater, diving beetles breathe air that they trap in a special area under the wing cases.

Water beetles

Diving beetles live in rivers and lakes and swim by using their fringed back legs like oars. They are hunters and catch prey such as other insects and even small fish. They lay their eggs in water, and these hatch into predatory larvae.

PARASITES

A parasite lives on or in another animal—the host—taking food from its body.

Fleas There are more than 2,000 species of fleas, and all have piercing mouthparts for sucking blood from the animals they live on. Fleas belong to a separate group of insects from bugs and beetles.

Cat flea

Bedbugs These parasitic bugs don't live on their hosts but in their nest—or bed—and come out at night to feed on blood. Bedbugs are only about 0.15 inches (4 mm) long and can run very fast. They are believed to be able to go without food for as long as a year.

Bedbug

Gardener's friend

The ladybug is a kind of beetle. It is much loved by gardeners because both adults and their young feed on sap-sucking aphids. The ladybug's bright colors warn potential predators that it can give off a nasty-tasting substance if attacked.

Noisy bugs

Cicadas are probably the noisiest of all bugs. They make their buzzing sound by vibrating drumlike structures on the body with special muscles. Only males sing, and each species has a slightly different song.

Water bugs

The largest of the bugs are these giant water bugs, which are often 2 inches (6 cm) long and can grow to an amazing 4 inches (10 cm). They swim with their back legs and use their front legs to catch prey, such as other insects and fish.

Boring beetle

Weevils are also known as snout beetles because of their long, beaklike snouts. They feed on plants and use their snout to bore into stems, flower buds, and seedpods, often destroying the plant in the process. Many kinds of weevils are serious pests of food crops.

Plant eaters

Aphids are tiny bugs, up to 0.3 inches (8 mm) long, that feed on the sap of many kinds of plants. They reproduce very quickly, so they occur in large numbers and can do serious damage to plants. Aphids also excrete a sweet liquid, called honeydew, that some other insects like to feed on.

GIANT BEETLE

At up to 7 inches (18 cm) long, Hercules beetles are among the largest in the world.

These mighty beetles live in rain forests in Central and South America. They are plant eaters and feed mostly on fruit, tree sap, and other plant matter. The larvae often live in tree stumps and feed on decaying wood.

The male has long horns and is also known as the rhinoceros beetle.

DID YOU KNOW? Most bugs lay eggs, but aphids can give birth to live young.

Bees, wasps, and ants

Some of the most important, familiar, and useful of all insects belong to this group. For example, they pollinate plants and help to control other types of insects by preying on them. Many live alone, but ants and some kinds of bees and wasps form large groups called colonies. The colony is ruled by one female, the queen, who lays all the eggs, while the rest of the insects gather food, build the nest, and care for the young.

It is said that honeybees must visit as many as two million flowers to make 1 pound (0.5 kg) of honey.

Honeybees

Worker bees fly out from the nest to gather pollen and nectar from flowers. As they do so, they transfer pollen from plant to plant—they are the most important of all pollinators. The bees use pollen as food for their young and nectar for making honey.

LIVING STORAGE POTS

When food is plentiful, honeypot ants use some of their workers to store food.

These workers eat so much nectar that their abdomens swell up to the size of small grapes. These ants cannot move but simply hang in the nest like storage pots. When food is scarce, these ants regurgitate food for the rest of the colony.

A honeypot ant with its swollen abdomen full of nectar

Leaf-cutter ants

These ants live in tropical rain forests. They cut pieces of leaves up to 20 times their own weight and carry them back to their nest. The ants use the leaves as a compost for growing fungus, which they then eat.

TERMITES

These insects are in a separate group from ants and bees, but they also live in colonies.

Egg layer As with ants, a large queen termite rules the colony. She lays as many as 30,000 eggs a day.

Termite mound

Queen termite surrounded by workers

Nest Termites make football-shaped nests in trees, but they also build complex underground homes. These have chambers for storing food and raising young and a special area for the queen. The large mound above the nest is like a chimney. It acts as a kind of air-conditioning system to keep the nest cool and well aired.

The ichneumon wasp drives her long egg-laying tube into wood and lays her eggs.

Wasp lifestyles

Common wasps live in colonies. Adults feed mostly on nectar and fruit, but they catch other insects to feed their young. They kill prey with the sharp stinger at the end of the body. Parasitic wasps, such as the ichneumon, live alone. They lay their eggs near the larvae of other insects, and the young wasps feed on these when they hatch.

Ferocious ants

Bulldog ants are perhaps the most dangerous and aggressive of all ants and have a deadly sting. An ant can hold onto an attacker with its strong jaws and inject venom with the long stinger on its abdomen.

DID YOU KNOW? Bulldog worker ants can be up to 1.5 inches (3.7 cm) long!

Flies

Buzzing flies can be annoying, and some carry deadly diseases, but they do have their uses. They are important pollinators of plants; food for many other creatures; and, as larvae, processors of waste matter. Flies live everywhere—there are even two kinds of midges in Antarctica. They are fast, agile flyers, but they have only one pair of wings. The other wings have become small knobbed structures called halteres that help a fly balance in the air.

Gadfly

A horsefly's eyes are made up of thousands of tiny lenses, or facets.

Bloodsucker

A horsefly has a stout body and huge eyes. Males feed mostly on flower nectar, but females need more protein so they can produce eggs. They feed on blood from animals, including humans, and can give a nasty bite.

DANGEROUS FLIES

Certain kinds of mosquitoes are probably the most dangerous of all animals because they carry a deadly disease called malaria.

Fast flyers Mosquitoes beat their wings so fast that they make a whining sound, and they are more often heard than seen. Males eat plant nectar and sap, but most females are blood feeders. They bite vertebrate animals, including people, and suck their blood. They can transmit disease as they do so.

Female mosquito

Eggs and the young
Mosquitoes lay their eggs in water. They hatch into larvae, which feed and grow in water.

Mosquito larvae

Crane fly larva

Life cycle

Most flies, including long-legged crane flies, lay eggs, which hatch into soft, legless larvae known as maggots. Crane fly larvae live in soil and feed on plants, but some fly larvae prey on the young of other insects. Other larvae live as parasites inside the bodies of other creatures.

Butterflies and moths

Beautiful, colorful butterflies and moths are the second-largest group of insects. All have big eyes, tubelike mouthparts for sucking up liquid food, and two pairs of wings with a covering of tiny scales. Their eggs hatch into larvae called caterpillars, which have chewing mouthparts. A caterpillar feeds constantly on plants and grows fast until it is large enough to become a pupa. It then make the transformation into an adult butterfly or moth.

Monarch butterfly

When a caterpillar is fully grown, it makes a hard case around itself and becomes a pupa (see far left, above). Inside this case, its body breaks down and re-forms. It emerges as a winged butterfly.

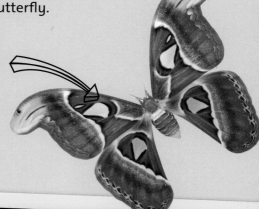

The Atlas moth has transparent patches on its wings, like windows.

Hummingbird moth

The hummingbird hawk moth has such a stout little body that it is easily mistaken for a tiny bird as it hovers in front of flowers, feeding on nectar. It beats its wings so fast that it makes a humming sound, just like its namesake. Its long mouthparts allow it to feed on deep flowers, such as honeysuckle.

GIANT MOTH

The Atlas moth is one of the largest moths with a wingspan of up to 10 inches (25 cm).

The moth lays its eggs on the underside of leaves, and they hatch into plump caterpillars that grow up to 4.7 inches (12 cm) long. The caterpillar has little spines all over its body, which are covered in a white waxy substance.

Atlas caterpillar

DID YOU KNOW? The emperor moth's feathery antennae can detect a female from 3 miles (5 km) away!

Mimicry and camouflage

Insects and spiders need to keep out of sight for two main reasons. First, many are food for other creatures and they want to avoid being caught. Second, by staying hidden, a predatory insect or spider can creep up on its own prey. Some, such as stick insects and leaf insects, manage to hide by looking extraordinarily like the twigs and leaves they live among, and they are very hard for predators to spot. This is called camouflage. Other insects resemble an object, such as a thorn, that is not attractive to predators, while others mimic other more dangerous creatures to deter potential attackers.

Wasp-mimic beetle

Look-alikes

Many animals associate black and yellow stripes with stinging wasps and an antlike body shape with the possibility of a nasty bite. By mimicking these dangerous creatures, harmless insects and spiders can gain some protection from predators.

Masters of disguise

Colorful crab spiders blend perfectly with bright flowers as the spiders lie in wait for prey. Some can even change color to match whatever flower they land on. The orchid mantis is even more extraordinary and matches the flower in shape and color.

This caterpillar looks so like a bird dropping that most predators will pass it by.

Crab spider

Ant-mimic spider

Thornbugs

Leaf insect

Mimicking nature

The spiky body of a thornbug is almost impossible to tell from a real thorn as the insect clings to a twig. Only when it moves does it give itself away. A leaf insect's camouflage is so perfect that it even has veinlike markings and patches that look as though they have been nibbled and are dying.

The four back legs of the orchid mantis are shaped like delicate flower petals.

Spiders and scorpions

Despite their fearsome reputation, only a few spiders are dangerous to people. They are predators, however, and they feed on huge numbers of insects. Spiders and scorpions are not insects but belong to a group of invertebrates called arachnids, which have eight legs and no wings or antennae. All spiders can make silk from glands at the end of their bodies, but not all make webs. They use silk to make other kinds of traps and to line burrows. The arachnid group also contains tiny creatures called mites and ticks, some of which live as parasites on other animals.

Weaving a web

The orb-weaving spider starts its web by making a framework of silken threads attached to supports, then adds spokes radiating from the center. Finally, it spins a spiral of sticky silk that will trap prey.

The scorpion's sting is linked to a venom gland at the end of its tail. To sting, the scorpion swings its tail over its body.

Scorpion carrying young

Scorpions

The scorpion seizes prey in its huge pincers, then, if necessary, injects it with venom from the stinger at the end of its tail. The female is a surprisingly attentive mother and carries her young around with her on her back.

LIFE IN A BUBBLE

The water spider spends its whole life in water.

It spins a bell-shaped underwater nest from silk and fills it with air bubbles that it brings back from the surface. The bubbles are trapped in the hairs on the spider's body.

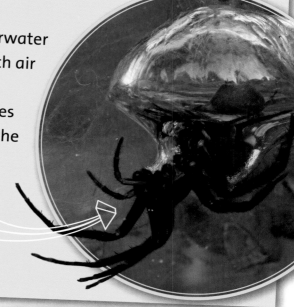

The spider catches tadpoles and insects that come close to the bell.

Clever trap

The trap-door spider lives in a burrow with a hinged lid made of silk. Silken tripwires all around the burrow are linked to the lid. If prey wanders into a tripwire, the spider springs out and grabs its victim in an instant.

The goliath bird-eating spider is the heaviest of all spiders, weighing up to 6 ounces (175 g).

CENTIPEDES

Centipedes are related to insects and spiders, but centipedes are in a separate group of invertebrates.

Many legs A centipede has a long, flattened body with a large number of legs—one pair for every segment of the body. The name means "100 legs," but most centipedes have far fewer, although one species that lives in Fiji has as many as 191 pairs of legs.

Lifestyle Centipedes generally live on the ground under rocks or logs or in buildings under floorboards and boxes. They are usually active at night and prey on insects and spiders, which they kill with a bite from their venomous fangs.

Centipede

Giant spider

Although the mighty goliath bird-eating spider can eat birds, it usually hunts insects and other small creatures such as mice, lizards, and frogs. It warns off enemies with a hissing noise and also flicks barbed hairs from its legs. These can cause severe irritation and breathing difficulties.

Crustaceans

Creatures as varied as lobsters, shrimp, barnacles, and woodlice all belong to the group of invertebrates called crustaceans. Most live in water, particularly the sea, but woodlice live on land. A typical crustacean has a tough outer shell, called an exoskeleton, which protects its soft body. On its head are two pairs of sensitive antennae, which help it find out about its surroundings. Attached to the body are a number of leglike appendages.

Barnacles

Goose barnacle eggs hatch into swimming larvae. Each larva then attaches itself via a stalk to a rock or a floating object such as a log or a boat and never moves again. To feed, a barnacle opens its shell and extends its feathery arms to collect tiny food items from the water.

Goose barnacle feeding

Giant crabs

The biggest of all the crustaceans is the Japanese spider crab. Its body measures only about 1 foot (30 cm), but it has very long spindly legs—like a spider—and weighs up to about 40 pounds (18 kg). It lives in waters off the coast of Japan and preys on other sea creatures.

LAND CRUSTACEANS

Woodlice usually live on damp ground, often under logs, flowerpots, and stones.

Staying safe These little crustaceans feed on rotting plant matter. Many creatures eat woodlice, and when in danger, a woodlouse grips the ground very tightly with its feet. One species, the pill woodlouse, has an even more effective means of defense—it rolls itself into a tight ball.

Pill woodlouse

Eggs and the young The female keeps her developing eggs in a special brood pouch on her body. The young emerge as mini versions of their mother and molt several times as they grow.

Common woodlouse

A Japanese spider crab's long legs can span up to 12 feet (3.6 m)—enough to straddle a car!

Echinoderms

Spiky sea urchins and colorful starfish are just some of the animals in this group, all of which live in the sea. Most have a body that is divided into five parts, with a mouth at the center. Some echinoderms, such as sea lilies, live attached to one spot by a stalk, but sea urchins and others move on tiny legs. These are called tube feet and are tipped with suction discs. The echinoderms move their tube feet by pumping water in and out of them.

SEA CUCUMBERS

These long-bodied creatures usually live on the seabed.

At one end of the sea cucumber is its mouth, surrounded by tentacles (actually modified tube feet), and at the other is its anus. This echinoderm feeds on tiny animals and plants that it takes from the water with its tentacles.

The sea cucumber can give off sticky threads to deter enemies.

Starfish

There are at least 2,000 kinds of starfish, or sea stars. They prey on other sea creatures such as clams and can open their shells with their tube feet. A starfish can also push its stomach out through its mouth to digest prey, then take it in again.

Red sea star

Blue linckia sea star

Crown-of-thorns starfish

Sea urchins

Many kinds of sea urchins have long spines and live on rocks on the seabed. They crawl around on their tube feet, searching for algae and small animals to eat. But not all sea urchins are spiky. Sand dollars have a flattened body and very short spines. They live buried in sand.

DID YOU KNOW? Brittle stars can grow new arms if damaged!

Mollusks

These creatures live in the sea and freshwater as well as on land and are some of the most familiar of all invertebrates. There are three main groups of mollusks: the gastropods, which include snails, slugs, and limpets; bivalves, such as clams, mussels, and scallops; and cephalopods—squid, cuttlefish, and octopuses. Molluscs have a wide range of body shapes, but many have a shell that protects the soft body. A typical mollusk also has a "foot" at the base of the body. This is a fleshy muscular structure on which the animal can move along.

Opalescent sea slug

Sea-living slugs

Sea slugs are some of the most colorful animals in the sea, and many have horns and feathery gills on their body. Most live in tropical seas and crawl around the seabed, feeding on creatures such as sponges, corals, and barnacles. Sea slugs can grow up to 1 foot (30 cm) long.

The reef octopus weighs up to 5 pounds (1.5 kg), and its arms measure 2 feet (60 cm) or more.

Reef octopus

JET PROPULSION

Squid are among the speediest and most intelligent of all invertebrate animals.

Moving fast Squid have a long, torpedo-shaped body; eight arms; and two tentacles, used for catching prey. Squid move by a form of jet propulsion. They suck water into their body and shoot it out again, propelling themselves backward.

Squid eye

Amazing eyes Squid and other cephalopods have the most advanced eyes of any invertebrates. They are quite similar to mammal eyes, with a retina, a lens, an iris, and a pupil.

Atlantic longfin squid

Loch's chromodoris sea slug

Land snails

A land snail has a hard shell to protect its soft body, and it can pull its head inside the shell if in danger. Its fleshy foot makes mucus to help it glide along, and the snail leaves a slimy trail behind it. A land snail breathes air through a tiny hole in its side.

SWIMMING SCALLOPS!

Many mollusks stay in one place or move very slowly, but scallops can swim surprisingly quickly!

A scallop has two hard shells protecting its soft body. To swim, it claps its shells together, pushing out jets of water that move it forward.

There are up to 100 eyes around the edge of the scallop's body.

Giant mollusk

The giant clam is the biggest of all the mollusks. It can grow up to 4 feet (1.2 m) long and weighs 500 pounds (230 kg) or more. It feeds by filtering plankton from the water but also uses energy produced by the algae (tiny plants) that live inside its body.

Color change

The octopus has a large pouchlike body and eight long arms, each lined with two rows of strong suckers. Like the squid, it can move by jet propulsion, but it can also crawl over the seabed on its long arms. It spends much of its time hiding from predators— and prey—and can quickly change color to match its surroundings.

Blue-ringed octopus

DID YOU KNOW? The blue-ringed octopus is one of the most venomous of all sea creatures!

Jellyfish, worms, and sponges

These creatures are some of the simplest of all animals, but even sponges need to catch food and reproduce, just like more complex creatures. Jellyfish and sea anemones belong to a group called cnidarians. Most have tube- or bell-shaped bodies and tentacles equipped with stinging cells. Many worms, such as earthworms, have segmented bodies, but flatworms have a simple flattened shape. Some live as parasites inside other animals, but others live in the sea and in freshwater.

Lion's mane jellyfish

This is the world's largest jellyfish. Its body can be more than 6 feet (2 m) wide, and its many tentacles may extend more than 100 feet (30 m). It preys on fish and other creatures, which it catches with its stinging tentacles.

The clown fish is protected by the sea anemone in return for allowing it to eat scraps of the prey the fish catches.

SPONGES

They might look like plants, but sponges are animals.

Sponges can reproduce from bits that break off existing animals, but they also lay eggs that hatch into swimming larvae. Adult sponges live fixed to one spot and feed by filtering water through the body. Any food particles are trapped and digested.

A stove-pipe sponge living next to a brain coral

Comb jellies

These little creatures have a simple bag-shaped body, which is lined with rows of tiny hairs called cilia. The animal beats these to move itself through the water as it searches for other small animals to catch and eat.

Cilia

A comb jelly has eight rows of many thousands of cilia.

Good partners

A sea anemone has a simple tube-shaped body with a central mouth that is surrounded by lots of tentacles. It uses these stinging tentacles to catch prey. The clown fish, however, can live among the tentacles unharmed.

Marine flatworms

As the name suggests, the body of a flatworm is flattened, not in segments like that of an earthworm. Because the body is so flat, the worm cannot swallow prey but can push out part of its gut to digest it outside the body.

MAN-OF-WAR

The Portuguese man-of-war is not a jellyfish but a colony of individual animals called polyps, which live together as one.

The float One member of the colony is the float, the gas-filled structure that sits on the surface of the water. Below that are tentacle polyps, which extend some 100 feet (30 m) to search for prey deep down in the water.

Close-up of tentacle

Feeding tentacles The tentacles are covered with tiny venom-filled stinging cells that are used to kill and paralyze prey. The tentacles contract to bring the prey up to special feeding polyps, which absorb and digest the food for the colony. There are also reproductive individuals that make eggs and sperm.

Portuguese man-of-war

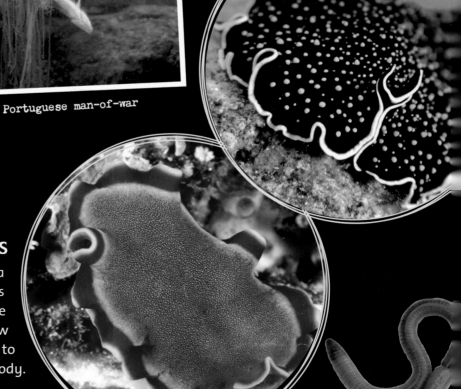

Index

Credits and Acknowledgments

Key tl=top left; t=top; tc=top center; tr=top right; cl=center left; c=center; cr=center right; bl=bottom left; bc=bottom center; br=bottom right; bg = background

ARD = Ardea; **ANT** = Australian Nature Transparencies; **COR** = Corel Corp.; **DT** = Dreamstime; **GI** = Getty Images; **iS** = istockphoto.com; **MP** = Minden Pictures; **NHPA** = NHPA/Photoshot; **NPL** = Nature Picture Library; **SH** = Shutterstock; **SP** = SeaPics; **TPL** = photolibrary.com.

Cover

Front cover: bg, c, cr, t, tl iS; br TPL. Back cover: cl, cr NHPA; bc TPL.

Photographs

1c NPL; **2**br, tr iS; cl SH; **2-3**bg iS; **3**c iS; **4**cr, tr iS; tl SH; **4-5**bc iS; **5**tl GI; bc iS; tc NPL; tr SH; **6** (Mammals) bl, br, cr iS; c, cl SH; **7** (Birds) tr NHPA; c, cr NPL; tl SH; **6-7** bg, t iS; **8** (Reptiles) br iS; bcl, bcr, tr SH; (Fish) c iS; bc, c, tl NPL; **9** (Amphibians) cl iS; tc NPL; bc, br SH; (Invertebrates) cl, cr, tc, tr iS; bcr, br, c, cr SH; **8-9** bg, t iS; **10-11**c TPL; **12**bc, bl iS; br NHPA; tc SH; tr TPL; **12-13**c iS; **13**tl ANT; tc iS; tr NPL; cr SH; br TPL; **14**cr, tr iS; c NPL; bc, br, cr, tl TPL; **15**bcr iS; bc, cr, tcr TPL; **16**bl, c iS; br SH; tr TPL; **17**bl, br, cr, tcr iS; tl NHPA; bcr TPL; **18**bl, c iS; tr NPL; **18-19**bc ARD; c NPL; **19**br, tc NHPA; tr NPL; **20**bl NHPA; bc SH; **20-21**bg NPL; **21**br NHPA; tc NPL; cl, tr TPL; **22**br, tr iS; bl NHPA; bc NPL; **22-23**c iS; **23**bl, tl iS; bc, br, tr NPL; **24**bc, bl iS; **24-25**cl TPL; **26**cr DT; bc, bl iS; br NPL; **26-27**tl NHPA; **27**bl, br, cr NPL; **28**bl SH; **28-29**c iS; **29**bc, br, tc iS; cr NPL; c SH; tr TPL; **30**br NHPA; bl, c TPL; **30-31**tl SH; **31**tc, tr NHPA; bl NPL; cr SH; c TPL; **32**cl, tr NPL; **32-33**bl TPL; **33**c, tc NPL; tr SH; br TPL; **34**bl TPL; **34-35**tc iS; bl NPL; **35**br, cl, tcr iS; bcr TPL; **36**bc, bl, c NPL; **36-37**bc SP; tr TPL; **37**br NPL; cl TPL; **38**bc NPL; br, tr SH; **39**bl, br NPL; c, tr TPL; **40**bcl iS; cr NPL; bl, c TPL; **40-41**tr NPL; c TPL; **41**br, tl NPL; c, cr SH; bl TPL; **42**cl, cr SH; bl TPL; **42-43**tc TPL; **43**r iS; bc NHPA; c NPL; cl SH; tc TPL; **44**bc, bl iS; **44-45**bc, c, tc TPL; **45**c GI; br NPL; **46**br iS; bl TPL; **46-47**t TPL; **47**br, cr, tc NPL; bcr SH; c TPL; **48-49**c TPL; **50**bl, c iS; tr TPL; **50-51**bc TPL; **51**bc, cl NPL; br, cr TPL; **52**bcl, tr iS; bcr NHPA; bl, cl, cr NPL; **53**bl iS; br, cl NPL; cr TPL; **54**bl iS; c NPL; **54-55**bc NPL; tc SH; **55**tr iS; cr SH; c TPL; **56**tr iS; bl TPL; **56-57**bc SH; bg iS; **57**bcr, tc, tcr iS; bc MP; **58-59**bg NPL; **59**bl, br iS; cl TPL; **59**bc iS; bcr NHPA; tcr TPL; **60**bl, tr TPL; **60-61**bg TPL; **61**cr, tr NPL; br TPL; **62**tr iS; bl NPL; cl SH; br TPL; **62-63**cl NPL; **63**c iS; b NPL; tl SH; tr TPL; **64**bl, cr iS; **64-65**tc NPL; **65**br, cl, cr NPL; tr TPL; **66**bl, cr NPL; tr TPL; **66-67**tc NHPA; **67**tc MP; c, r NPL; br TPL; **68**bl GI; c iS; **68-69**bg, c GI; **69**c GI; bc iS; tr MP; **70**tr iS; br SH; bl, cl TPL; **70-71**bc NPL; tc SH; **71**br MP; c, tr NPL; tl TPL; **72**cl iS; bl, cr, tc, tr NPL; **73**tl NHPA; bl, tr NPL; **74-75** GI; **76**br NHPA; bc NPL; **76-77**tc GI; tc NPL; **77**c iS; cr NHPA; bc, tc, tr NPL; **78-79**tl NPL; c SH; **78**br iS; bc NPL; **79**br, tr NPL; **80**tl, tr GI; bl, cr NHPA; c NPL; **81**bl, cl NHPA; br, tr NPL; **82**bl, tr GI; br iS; tc NHPA; bc NPL; **83**bl, cl GI; c iS; tr NPL; **84**bl, br GI; tr NPL; **84-85**r iS; **85**cr iS; **86**c, tr iS; bl SH; **86-87**bc NHPA; r, tc NPL; **87**cr, tc NPL; **88**tr iS; bc NPL; **88-89**tc iS; c NHPA; **89**bcl, br NHPA; bc, cr, tc NPL; **90**bc, br NPL; **90-91**tc iS; **91**bcr GI; tcr iS; cl NHPA; br NPL; **92**cr GI; tc iS; bc NHPA; tr NPL; **92-93**tc NPL; **93**c, cl GI; cr, tc iS; br, tr NHPA; **94-95**c GI; **96**bl iS; **96-97**bc, tc NPL; **97**tr GI; c, cl iS; tl NPL; br SH; **98**br, tr iS; bc, c NPL; **99**bl, cl GI; cr, tr NPL; **100**cl SH; bc SP; **100-101**tr GI; bc iS; **101**cr SH; tc SP; **102**bcr GI; bl, tcr NHPA; tr SH; **102-103**bc GI; **103**tr NHPA; bc, cl NPL; **104**bl GI; **104-105**bc, tc NHPA; c SP; **105**c iS; br, tl NPL; tr SH; **106**c NPL; bl SH; cl SP; **106-107**bc, bg NPL; **107**br, c NPL; bc SP; **108-109** iS; **110**bc iS; **110-111**tc iS; **111**cl GI; br iS; bc NHPA; c NPL; tc, tr SH; **112**bl COR; c GI; br iS; cl SH; **112-113**c GI; bc, tc NPL; **113**br, tl NHPA; tr SH; **114**bc NHPA; **114-115**tc iS; bc SH; **115**br, cl GI; cr iS; tl NPL; c SH; **116**bcr iS; tcr, tr NPL; bcl, tcl SH; bc SPL; **116-117**bc NPL; **117**tcr, tr iS; bcr NPL; cl SH; **118**cl, tr NPL; bc SH; **118-119**tc iS; bg NPL; **119**tc NPL; cr SH; **120**bl, cr, tr NPL; **120-121**tc NPL; c SH; **121**bc, cr GI; br NHPA; **122**cl, tr NHPA; bc, cl SH; **122-123**bc GI; **123**br iS; bc, bl, cl, cr, tc SH; **124**bl GI; c NPL; tr SH; **124-125**bc iS; tc SH; **125**br GI; c, cr NPL; tc SH; **126**tr GI; bc SH; **126-127**bc GI; **127**c, cl, tc GI; br iS; bc NHPA; tr NPL; cr SH; **128**bc iS; **128-129**tc iS; **129**br iS; **130**bc iS; **130-131**tc NHPA; **131**br iS.

Repeated images courtesy of iStockphoto.com.

Illustrations

All illustrations copyright Weldon Owen Publishing Ltd.